NAUGHTY
NEW YORK

A Lady's Guide to the Sexy City

NAUGHTY NEW YORK

A Lady's Guide to the Sexy City

FLEUR DE LIRE PRESS

NAUGHTY NEW YORK
A LADY'S GUIDE TO THE SEXY CITY
Edited by Heather Stimmler-Hall

Photos by Kirsten Loop

www.naughtynewyorkguide.com

First Edition, 2012
ISBN 978-2-9531870-2-1 (print)
ISBN 978-2-9531870-3-8 (eBook)

CAVEAT EMPTOR

As much as we like to think we were exhaustive in our research, places close, times change, obnoxious lowlifes get admitted into our favorite clubs and the Artful Dodger strikes just when you've purchased that darling new clutch purse. The author and publisher of Naughty New York cannot accept responsibility for facts that become outdated, wardrobe failure, or for any inadvertent errors or omissions in this guide. Confirm in advance when it matters.

Published in France by
Fleur de Lire Press
77 avenue des Gobelins
75013, Paris
www.fleurdelire.com

Designed by *the*BookDesigners, www.bookdesigners.com
Printed and bound in China

Dépôt légal: janvier 2012
Imprimé en Chine

CONTENTS

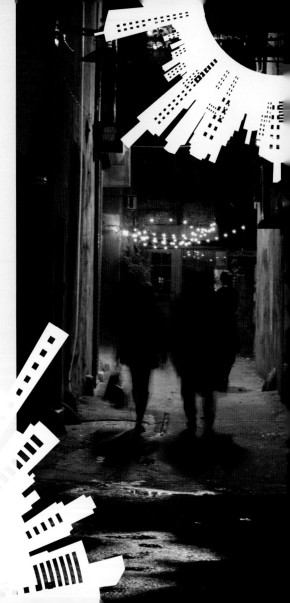

PART I

New York, New York

IS THIS GUIDE FOR YOU?

"If Paris is about sensual pleasure,
New York is about freedom."

Sex. Power. Culture. Success. New York City thrives on this heady cocktail like no other place in the world, fueling its legendary energy with an electric undercurrent of our collective hopes, dreams, and fantasies. It's the ultimate epicenter of intellect and desire, indulgence and independence, the forbidden and the formidable.

True, the bright lights of this big city can sometimes shine coldly upon the countless millions who come expecting a warmer welcome. Don't take it personally. New York City may be indifferent, but it's never judgmental. And therein lies one of its most alluring traits. For women, this glittering metropolis seduces us with promises of adventure, opportunity, excitement....and the freedom to have a bit of naughty fun.

Because if Paris is about sensual pleasure, New York is about freedom. The freedom to experience pleasure on your own terms. To define your own womanhood. Your own sexuality. In New York, naughtiness isn't about living up to someone else's expectations. It's about making your own rules, testing your own taboos, and indulging in self-gratification with no excuses and no apologies.

Once you're ready to take your bite out of the Big Apple, rest assured there's no need to waste your own precious time figuring out the best way to board this fast-moving train. *Naughty New York* is your passport to the sexy side of the city, written by a talented team of local ladies diverse in age, lifestyle, expertise, and zip code. Whether you're a newcomer or know Manhattan like the back of your hand, these useful insider tips, carefully vetted secret addresses, and female-friendly recommendations will help you discover the best of what's sexy, sultry, suggestive...and downright naughty!

Naughty Definition

Self-gratification, n. The act of giving oneself pleasure or of satisfying one's own desires.

NAUGHTY...BUT NICE

*"If you obey all the rules,
you miss all the fun."* —KATHARINE HEPBURN

Naughty New York is first and foremost a lady's guide. It reveals a sexy and provocative city seen through the eyes of the fairer sex. You won't find anything nasty, illegal or disrespectful between these sheets. A lady's guide has no place for brothels, escorts, or peep shows. This is not a manual for getting lucky, nor is it the last word on sex in this city. If you're already well-initiated in the "lifestyle" you may find Naughty New York charmingly tame. If you're the kind of woman who blushes in the lingerie department, then you might find it positively shocking.

This guide is simply a taste of the many delights New York has to offer to discerning ladies, whether you want to feel the thrill of being laced up in a corset, the titillation of a neo-burlesque show, or the seduction of a handsome stranger at a sex party. Not that you should feel pressured into wanton debauchery. You're also free to merely enjoy the sights from the sidelines. But we think you'll find it hard to resist Manhattan's contagious energy for long. If Paris is about *laissez-faire*, New York is about making it happen. And with the information you find in this guide, you've got the freedom to choose your own adventure…naughty *or* nice.

"New York is a galaxy of adventure at once elegant, exciting and bizarre. It's a city that moves so fast, it takes energy just to stand still."

—BARBARA WALTERS

THREE WAYS TO
ENJOY NAUGHTY NEW YORK

"*Get ready to be the sex goddess
you always knew you could be.*"

Solo

 ew York City is where women learned to master the iconic art of being sexy, sophisticated and single. It's the prime venue for both liberation and safe self-realization. The New York woman wouldn't dare take on the world alone without a well-edited address book of the city's exclusive and beloved shops, salons, parks, bars and restaurants, honed through practice and special attention to detail. Naughty New York shares these secrets with all the single ladies who unapologetically expect only the best.

With the Ladies

New York City is a girlfriends' playground; the ideal place to satiate your naughty curiosities and thrill your senses with your closest confidantes. Whether on a simple girls' weekend or a bachelorette's last hurrah, Naughty New York will inspire your wild side and reveal the best way for your circle to take on the city. With an array of activities that inspire and challenge one's concepts of propriety, even the world's wildest bridesmaid will find her bliss while not comprising the (not so) blushing bride.

With Your Man

Naughty New York is the discerning guide to living out your naughtiest fantasies with the man in your life, whether you're celebrating 20 years of marriage or 20 minutes of shameless flirting. We help you find the sexiest hotel suites, the most intimate restaurants, the best tantric sex classes and the most exclusive "couples only" parties. Get ready to be the sex goddess you always knew you could be.

NAUGHTY
NEW YORK HISTORY

"Gotham's women did something naughtier
than breaking the rules: they changed them."

While Parisians preferred discretion and Londoners practiced restraint, bold New Yorkers have always thrived on naughty notoriety, promoting and profiting from saucy spectacles and erotic entertainment.

In 1896, one of the very first films ever made was a scandalous 20-second production by Thomas Edison called *The Kiss*, where May Irwin and John Rice reenacted a lingering embrace from their 1895 Broadway play *The Widow Jones*. Although decidedly G-rated by today's standards, at the time its racy reputation made it one of the first box-office hits in Times Square.

> *"Between two evils, I always choose the one I've never tried before."*
>
> —*MAE WEST*

Three decades later the sassy, wise-cracking Broadway actress Mae West catapulted herself into stardom after being arrested for her play *Sex*, which featured a "prostitute with a heart of gold." She followed up on the free publicity stunt a year later with the 1928 production of *The Pleasure Man*, another controversial play filled with Brooklyn street slang and "loose morals" that was forced to close down because of public decency laws.

Rather than allow Puritanical hypocrisy and outdated social taboos to cramp their style, Gotham's women did something even naughtier than breaking the rules: they changed them. New York City has been the frontline of America's sexual (r)evolution for over a century. Long before *Sex & the City* glamorized the lives of four fictional Manhattan ladies and their stiletto shopping, Cosmo sipping, and boyfriend chasing antics, real New York women fought the battles for sexual, political, and economic equality that would change the lives of women everywhere.

> *"There is something in the New York air that makes sleep useless. Perhaps it is that the heart beats faster here than elsewhere."*
>
> —*SIMONE DE BEAUVOIR*

> *"When I left the West Coast I was a liberal. When I landed in New York I was a revolutionary."*
>
> —*JANE FONDA*

New York World correspondent Nellie Bly shunned fashion and entertainment assignments to report on topics such as the plight of female factory workers in the 1880s, and going as far as feigning insanity to investigate conditions inside an asylum. In 1909 Carrie Chapman Catt organized the New York City Women's Suffrage Party, and in 1920 became president of the League of Women Voters after the successful passage of the 19th amendment. In 1923 Margaret Sanger opened the first birth control clinic in Greenwich Village (now home to the Bleeker Street Planned Parenthood Clinic) after smuggling Dutch diaphragms into the country inside bootleg gin crates. Feminist journalist Gloria Steinem went undercover in 1963 as a Playboy Bunny at Manhattan's Playboy Club and in 1972 co-founded the ground-breaking *Ms.* Magazine.

BEST PLAY
2008 TONY AWARD · PULITZER PRIZE
AUGUST: OSAGE COUNTY
BILLY ELLIOT
THE MUSICAL
ELTON JOHN
LEE HALL
STEPHEN DALDRY
IN THE HEIGHTS
2008 TONY AWARD
BEST MUSICAL
TICKETMASTER.COM
212-307-4100
InTheHeightsTheMusical.com
nycgo.com
THOMSON REUTERS
FOREX
CROSS RATES
EUR VS JPY
115.7500
CTRL GOVT'S 2009
Morgan Stanley
Reese's
ROXY
City Sights NY
tkts

On New York Men

> *"If you see a New York man who tickles your fancy, do not hesitate to walk up and offer to buy him a drink."*

Who are New York men?

Whether he is a native New Yorker or just arrived from the remote recesses of Bujumbura to conquer Manhattan, the man who makes his home in New York is a special breed. It is a unique type of male who comes to this city to get something, prove something, to conquer something. Possessed with an insatiable hunger, these men take the A-Type personality to new heights. Not content to merely outdo all their Oxbridge or Harvard classmates, they strive for success on the level of Caesar or Genghis Khan, constantly raising the bar in their domain. When it comes to women, they can be fearsome.

Mental Attributes

Though the New York man often has a strong – even overwhelming – physical presence, what is most important (and most attractive) is his mind. New York men are not always conventionally good-looking. The stereotype of a short, pudgy man next to a blond, svelte bombshell half his age often rings true in New York. A man's wallet may be the impetus behind this pairing, but the secret weapon behind his wallet is his mind. Unlike London, breeding in New York is of no consequence. Unlike Paris, savoir-vivre holds no currency. Raw intellectual excellence and its resulting success – no matter how it is procured – is the New York man's calling card. His intellect makes the New York man insatiable for information (as well as other lurid appetites). Women may find it infuriating that he can be seen talking on the phone, running on the treadmill, looking at his other blackberry, keeping one eye on the television, and talking to his friend who is doing exactly the same thing next him at the same time, but it's also part of what makes him so intriguing. Note well that these men may value intellect and the success it brings them, but this doesn't apply when sizing up the opposite sex. New York men can be as shallow as the next man, seeking out first and foremost aesthetic beauty in their women.

ARCHETYPES

The Entrepreneur, The Intellectual, The Artist and The Working Man.

ALTHOUGH NEW YORK MEN ARE DIVERSE IN EVERY WAY, MOST OF THE ONES YOU MEET CAN FALL INTO ONE OF THESE FOUR CATEGORIES. WHETHER THEY ARE MASTERS OF FORTUNE OR STRUGGLING ARTISTS, TRADITIONAL OR AVANT GARDE, METRO-SEXUAL OR UNAPOLOGETICALLY RUGGED (OR IN DESPERATE NEED OF A SHAVE), NEW YORK MEN ARE AT THE CUSP OF THEIR FIELD, SETTING NEW STANDARDS AND WRITING NEW RULES. THIS IS WHAT MAKES THEM FASCINATING AND SEXY. WHATEVER YOUR ICONIC NEW YORK MALE FANTASY, KNOW THAT HE IS HERE AND HE IS READY TO TAKE ON THE WORLD.

THE ENTREPRENEUR: What they have to offer women is the best of the best, materially speaking. Think Michael Douglas' character Gordon Gecko in *Wall Street*: always impeccably dressed in bespoke suits and shirts, car and driver always at the ready, a jet available at any moment, a reservation at any table in the city and a seat at any show. They aim to impress, to awe, to seduce. A typical date may involve drinks at a trendy bar, a show on Broadway, dinner at an exclusive restaurant and dancing at a private club. Helicopter rides, champagne in the Presidential Suite at the end of the night and invitations to fly to the Cayman's for the weekend are *de rigueur*. They take the lead. They decide the agenda. And they pay. Other fictitious versions of the Entrepreneur include Humphrey Bogart's Linus Larabee in *Sabrina*, Tom Hanks' Joe Fox in *You've Got Mail*, Christian Bale's Patrick Bateman in *American Psycho*. Real versions of the Entrepreneur include Michael Bloomberg and Jared Kushner.

THE INTELLECTUAL: The New York intellectual is tortured, neurotic, brilliant and discursive. Woody Allen incarnates the iconic New York intellectual but Malcolm Gladwell and Andrew Ross Sorkin have a place in this Pantheon as well. Fictitious versions include John Cusak's Jonathan Trager in *Serendipity*, Ryan Reynolds' Will Hayes in *Definitely Maybe* and Billy Crystal's Harry Burns in *When Harry Met Sally*. If he's not working on his next book, he's promoting it on Charlie Rose, or attending an art opening in Chelsea and hanging out in local haunts on the Lower East Side. We desire them to be hopeless romantics, but even intellectuals in New York City are shrewd business men. Expect drinks at speak easy-type bars with hand cut ice in your drinks, some sort of post modern vampire-inspired opera in a basement or a performance art gig in Brooklyn before ending in a deli or the latest restaurant written up in *New York Magazine*.

THE ARTIST: The New York Artist may be sensitive, but he's no weakling. He has come to New York to make his mark on the world just as Andy Warhol, John Lennon and Basquiat before him. Though tortured and passionate, he is confident in the purpose of his creative vocation. And nothing will stand in his way. His penchant for the avant garde and spontaneous are only limited (or perhaps inspired) by the limits of his wallet. But if you are a woman who favors the aesthetic plane to the material one, then prepare for an adventure that will redefine your notions of intensity.

THE WORKING MAN: The Working Man can be a native New Yorker, whose emblematic "how ya doin" has real power to make you melt on the spot. He can also be foreign-born, with entre-preneurial aspirations for himself and a better life for his family. Working men – with a special callout to our favorites in uniform at the NYPD and NYFD – are the heart and blood of New York City and can endear it to you like no other. Expect romantic rides on the Staten Island Ferry, a hockey match or baseball game. Fictitious versions of the working man include Edward Burns' Mickey Fitzpatrick in *She's The One*, Nicolas Cage's Charlie Lang in *It Can Happen to You* and Matthew McConaughey's Benjamin Barry in *How to Lose a Guy in Ten Days*.

Buyers Beware

Kindness and altruistic generosity are not driving principles for many New York men. Like the tragically preoccupied Narcissus, authentic romanticism can be hard to come by (he's already in love with number one). Bad behavior can be truly atrocious. Don't assume he isn't married just because you don't see a ring. And don't be surprised if he's scheduled a date after yours. And drop the guy who is texting with his other dates while out with you. Even after an extraordinary date (that might include a trip to his bedroom), he may actually never call you again. This is part and parcel of the New York dating experience. Take it with a grain of salt and have empathy for the New York woman who is hoping to find a life partner.

"As only New Yorkers know, if you can get through the twilight, you'll live through the night."

—DOROTHY PARKER

Fast City. Fast Nights.

People go to bed quickly in New York, often sleeping together before they're willing to share basic intimate details (such as their last names). Illicit or random encounters occur often in New York, as well. There are dedicated websites and personal ads devoted to this sort of hook-up. If you get past lunch or drinks and into an actual offer for dinner or a night out, you have passed a significant threshold. If he offers to have you over to cook for you, he may well be considering a proposal. Whatever your fancy, New York is all about seizing your chance, embracing serendipity and jumping in head first. As long as you are true to yourself, you can have a brilliant time. Delayed gratification, be damned!

How to Get His Attention and How to Keep It *(for at least the weekend).*

A woman is irresistible to a New York man if she is confident, self-possessed and well dressed. A hint of perfume and light make-up are sexy, but don't over-do it. New York is all about subtlety and style. Pick one accessory to draw attention. Shoes say a lot as does your jewelry. A well chosen pair of boots have been known to

take a man down. If you see a New York man who tickles your fancy, do not hesitate to walk up and offer to buy him a drink. If he approaches you, eschew temptations to play the demure and shy maiden and if you like him, smile and tell him what you're drinking. If you're not interested, politely say as much.

Naughty Tip

When jockeying for a cab with a handsome stranger, offer to split it. Then strike up a conversation and leave your business card on the seat when you get out.

Making Contact

Many New Yorkers are used to walking around with a shield of armor on – that is, they have their guard up when riding public transportation or walking down the street. These are not places a lady would be smiling and making eye contact. In a city packed with so many people, it's difficult to be totally open to strangers at all times. Still, that doesn't mean that New Yorkers are closed off to flirtation. New York men will be more than happy to stop and give you directions if you ask. If someone isn't open to your overtures, don't let it deter you. Most New Yorkers will be more than happy to chat you up – that is, if you can get them to take off their iPods.

Missed Connections

It's not always easy to approach a good-looking stranger, so some New Yorkers rely on Missed Connections via Craigslist http://newyork.craigslist.org/mis/ to try and find the one that got away. For example: "Girl in the green sweater who smiled at me on the 6 train...I can't stop thinking about you." Who knows, one of them could be about you!

On New York Women

"New York women are the living incarnation of the post modern Femme Fatale."

Uncommon Excellence

New York women are ambitious, stylish, intelligent, fearless and sexy, and found in far more variations than Carrie, Samantha, Charlotte and Miranda. Indeed, the talents and depth of New York women are limitless and admirable. Whether they seek out a career in finance, law, medicine, diplomacy, acting, publishing, academia, journalism, fashion, art or counter-terrorism, these are women who have eschewed a traditional path to pursue a career in the center of the world. Succeeding in New York requires remarkable talent, perseverance, sense of purpose and an uncanny ability to withstand rejection, criticism, competition and heartbreak

along the way. That New York's women not only survive but thrive in this city is a testament to how extraordinary they really are. That they do it while looking fabulous is nothing short of amazing!

Trademark Characteristics

Some fashion stereotypes actually do apply. New York women are impeccably manicured and pedicured (take note on the sly and there will not be an un-manicured nail in sight); New York women are fit—they run marathons, they kick box, they do triathlons, they are yoga and Pilates masters; and most iconically, New York women keep Christian Louboutin, Manolo Blahnik and Jimmy Choo in business. Style and aesthetic proclivities vary when it comes to their hair and their wares, but be certain New York women live on the edge of style. If there's one common denominator, it would be that all New York women are invariably beautiful, even stunning. In terms of fitness, fashion, make-up and polish, they are the best versions of themselves in every circumstance.

"Most human beings are driven to seek security and comfort. But there is another group that can only thrive on change and the unexpected of New York."

—CATHLEEN NESBIT

Know Thyself

New York women, like their male counterparts, strive to be the best. Even the bohemian, post-modern hippie artist living in a fourth floor walk-up in Queens is not one to simply coast along. To survive here, she has to want to be here. To thrive here, she has to know what she wants. New York City is the hub for the international cultural, intellectual, financial and diplomatic zeitgeist. And it's expensive. Being intelligent will only get you so far. Passion, ambition, and an ability to harness the frenetic energy that emanates from the very core of the city are essential. The New York woman also has to be deliberate and tough. Think Sigourney Weaver and Melanie Griffith in *Working Girl*, Parker Posey in *You've Got Mail*, and Meryl Streep in *The Devil Wears Prada*.

Are Men Really Necessary?

With self-knowledge comes a certain freedom and a real conviction of purpose. New York women have fashioned out for themselves a new standard for independence – sexually, financially, personally and professionally. It is consummate. These women recognize that many opportunities in this city are best achieved unshackled, and they celebrate that fact. Ariana Huffington's media career entered the stratosphere when she divorced Mike, and Padma Lakshmi gave up on Salman Rushdie once she took on *Top Chef*. New York women are the living incarnation of the post modern Femme Fatale: a woman whose desirability is greatly augmented by her autonomy, self-sufficiency and self-satisfaction. And though men may no longer be required in most circumstances, they are still desired...and hence acquired!

"My first few weeks in New York were an initiation into the kingdom of guts."
—SHIRLEY MACLAINE

Hidden Vulnerability

Though New York women are unforgiving and relentless in their pursuit for excellence, they still possess a hidden vulnerability. The challenges of urban living may have thickened their protective emotional shell, but once unmasked, naked and exposed, New York women are like all women. They desire tenderness, affection and love. This vulnerability is at the heart of a New York woman's inner beauty and sensuality. Though they are loath to expose any perceived weakness, the sexiest New York women navigate a higher plane where their strength and their fragility are openly revealed in tandem. Here, there is a tacit acknowledgement that one's power emerges from an ability to surrender oneself with true abandon to the forces and fates of life. And since we know that New York women risk it all to succeed, their hearts are no exception.

Urban Myths

There is a Holy Grail for New York women. It is the unobtainable Trifecta of possessing the perfect job, the perfect apartment and the perfect boyfriend all at the same time. There is a special place in heaven for women who excel in any one of these domains, let alone all three. And it is not only dependent on the woman, great luck and timing —serendipity if you will — are required as well. Many "unobtainables" can be added to this list: the perfect wardrobe, the perfect body, the perfect network, the perfect pair of shoes to go with the perfect Diane Von Furstenburg wrap dress. How do New York women persevere in such an unforgiving and perfectionist environment? The secret lies in her ability to determine her own standards of excellence and then to surpass them. The New York woman is defined by no one, not even other New York women. With this inner power, she does prevail: strong, vulnerable, independent, self-aware and fabulous!

To Know Her Is To (practically) Be Her

Emulating the New York woman means appropriating her City-savviness and self-possessiveness. In other words, you must exude confidence and entitlement (see the section on the Art of Hailing a Cab) and then surrender yourself to what New York City has to offer you. Finding your inner New Yorker is an exercise in personal empowerment for any woman, especially the woman traveling alone. But this is also an exercise in self-indulgence and play. Get a Manicure and Pedicure. Get your make-up done at Saks. Dress for the occasion. Select a destination and try your hand at living it up in the City.

Millionairesses of Manhattan

America's first female self-made millionaire was Sarah Breedlove, aka Madame CJ Walker (1867-1919), who marketed and sold beauty products for African-American women from her Harlem townhouse salon. Hetty Green, aka "The Witch of Wall Street" (1834-1916) turned a small inheritance into such a large fortune, through her shrewd investments and frugal living, that she was able to keep New York City afloat with a loan of $1.1 million during the Panic of 1907.

Naughty
NEW YoRK

A NEW YORK STATE OF MIND

> *New York women show they're ready to do whatever it takes to get what they want in Working Girl.*

Iconic Manhattan Movies

How to Marry a Millionaire (1953): Ambition, sex appeal, and elegance at its best as three models, Marilyn Monroe, Betty Grable, and Lauren Bacall, scheme to find the perfect husbands in Manhattan.

Breakfast at Tiffany's (1961): Audrey Hepburn's Holly Golightly shows how even Manhattan society girls with a hidden agenda can charm us with their touching vulnerability and defiant pride.

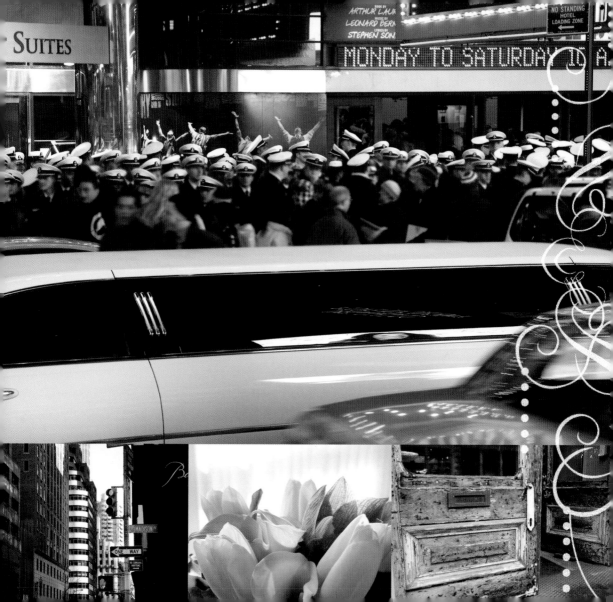

Funny Girl (1968): Barbara Streisand portrays the true-life rise to stardom of Fanny Brice, a Jewish girl from the Lower East Side who becomes one of the country's most influential comedic actresses of her time.

Annie Hall (1977): Diane Keaton was Woody Allen's inspiration for her signature role as the witty, neurotic, and androgynous free spirit Annie Hall. A tribute to the real magnetism of personal style.

Gloria (1980): In her role as Gloria, a tough-talking New Yorker helping protect her six-year-old neighbor from the mob, Gena Rowlands portrays a formidable older woman with a heart of gold and nerves of steel.

Desperately Seeking Susan (1985): This trashy, sexy, and hilarious comedy set in 1980's Manhattan will remind you how we all fell under Madonna's captivating spell.

A Chorus Line (1985): An engaging backstage peek into the ambitions, talent, passions, fragility and wit possessed by the diverse cast of characters trying to make it on Broadway. A powerful tale of big city dreams.

9 1/2 Weeks (1986): Kim Basinger and the once-handsome Mickey Rourke perform some of cinema's most memorable naughty scenes in this intense erotic drama about two New York strangers in the night.

Moonstruck (1987): When Cher's character as a 30-something Brooklyn bookkeeper admits she doesn't love her fiancée, her Italian mother played by Olympia Dukakis sagely replies, "Good. When you love them they drive you crazy because they know they can."

Working Girl (1988): Melanie Griffith comes across a sweetheart next to the ruthless Sigourney Weaver, but both of these New York women show they're ready to do whatever it takes to get what they want.

"I miss the animal buoyancy of New York, the animal vitality. I did not mind that it had no meaning and no depth."

—ANAIS NIN, FROM DIARIES, V. II

When Harry Met Sally (1989): Manhattan's scenery, Nora Ephron's witty dialog, and Harry Connick Jr's soundtrack make for a sap-free sentimental film about friendship, attraction…and how to fake an orgasm.

You've Got Mail (1998): A feisty indie bookstore owner who champions personalized customer interaction falls in love with an anonymous online suitor… who happens to own the book megastore around the corner. Only in Manhattan.

The Devil Wears Prada (2006): Fabulously coiffed and perfectly polished, Meryl Streep's stunning performance as the merciless, steely-eyed editor-in-chief of a famous New York fashion magazine saves this film from the damnation of chick-flick purgatory.

THE BIG APPLE ON THE SMALL SCREEN: Manhattan-based television series like *Friends*, *Seinfeld*, *Mad About You*, and *Will & Grace* may have introduced us to the human side of "everyday" New Yorkers, while series such as *30 Rock*, *Sex & the City*, and *Mad Men* present the more glamorous side of a very juicy Big Apple.

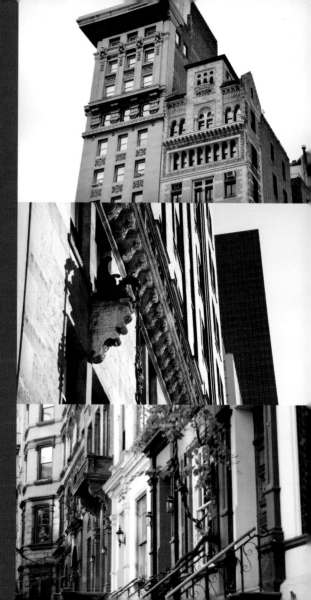

New York Literary Inspiration

The Age of Innocence by Edith Wharton (1920)
A portrait of upper class New York society in the 1870s, when the arrival of the passionate, independent-minded Countess Ellen Olenska threatens to ignite a family scandal.

Here is New York by E.B. White (1949)
The very essence of what makes New York City the greatest metropolis in the world is perfectly captured in this concise essay. White's loving observations of a city "both changeless and changing" ring true today.

Time and Again by Jack Finney (1970)
An illustrated Manhattan classic of an illustrator who travels in time back to 1882, falling in love with a beautiful young woman and a New York that no longer exists.

Dorothy Parker: What Fresh Hell Is This? by Marion Meade (1989)
An intriguing look into the tragic personal life of the sharp-witted writer and viciously humorous critic who frequented New York's famed Algonquin Round Table of notable writers and editors.

Writing New York: A Literary Anthology edited by Philip Lopate (2000)
Dip in and out of over 200 years of Gotham's literary past recounted through poetry, essays, fiction, diaries, and letters by 108 writers including Walt Whitman, Herman Melville, Henry Miller, and Willa Cather.

Garlic and Sapphires: The Secret Life of a Critic in Disguise by Ruth Reichl (2005)
With a mix of memories, recipes, and insider dirt from Manhattan's food world, this former New York Times restaurant critic dishes up a mouth-watering culinary adventure in the Big Apple.

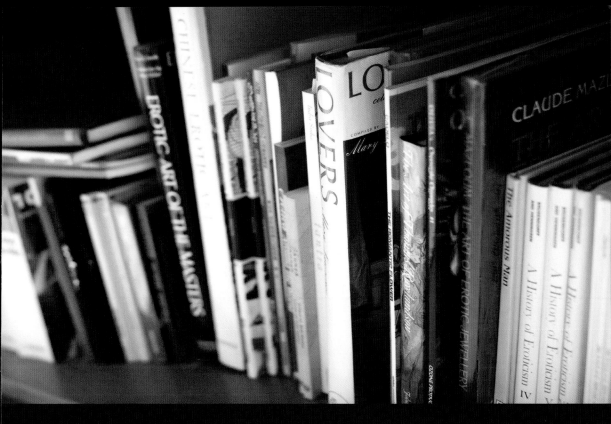

Why do they call it the Big Apple?

In 1924 the *New York Morning Telegraph* columnist John J. Fitz Gerald wrote "There's only one Big Apple. That's New York." Historians say he got the term from New Orleans horse racers who aspired to race in New York City's tracks, calling it the "Big Apple." The New York City tourism office adopted the Big Apple as their official logo in 1971, a wholesome and juicy symbol to entice more people to visit the city, which still suffered from its reputation as a dark and dangerous place.

PART II

Your Pad or Mine?
New York Accommodations

ACCOMMODATIONS

"No woman gets an orgasm from shining the kitchen floor." —BETTY FRIEDAN

B efore you dive into the racks at Barney's, before you start scoping out the best spot at that sexy cocktail bar, and even before you step one stilettoed foot in the Big Apple, you'll need to make a very important decision: where to stay. Sleeping beauties don't want to wake up on the wrong side of town, or in any bed that will get the day off to a bad start. Whether you choose a luxury hotel, a budget boutique, or rent a private apartment, this guide will help take the guesswork out of choosing the perfect one with our carefully-selected shortlist of centrally-located Manhattan establishments.

CHOOSING A HOTEL

"Woman's virtue is man's greatest invention." —CORNELIA OTIS SKINNER

Before you start comparing suites and amenities, decide what kind of experience you want to have in your New York hotel. Do you dream of a haven from the hustle and endless bustle of the city streets, where you sleep in luxurious peace and enjoy indulgent spa treatments? Or are you looking for a social HQ, a place where you can wine and dine, mingle with the locals and fellow travelers, and exchange meaningful glances with the charming concierge? Some hotels are all about the room, others are all about the public spaces. Some hotels are on quiet side streets, others are right off Times Square. Do you plan on spending most of your time in SoHo and the Meatpacking District, or Fifth Avenue and Central Park? Knowing this in advance, and choosing the hotel in the corresponding district, will save you time and taxi fares.

If you're the kind of guest who likes room service, dry cleaning, concierge services and attentive staff, choose the classic hotels over the trendy boutiques. Can't imagine skipping a luxurious bath or sharing a sensual shower? Beware of the old school industrial bathtub/shower combo – small, low, and uninspiringly shallow –still found in many hotels in NYC, even those otherwise completely renovated. Inspired by Gotham's gritty, badboy history? Even the slightly seedy budget dives can be sexy if you're into role playing, or need a place where your wild bachelorette party won't offend anyone. If you dream of stunning Manhattan skyline views, you'll need to request the upper floors in Midtown hotels, whereas SoHo and other lower Manhattan neighborhoods tend to have shorter buildings so a room on the 5th floor could have decent views.

Insider tip

Hotels know exactly how much each person has paid for their room, and whether they booked direct with the hotel itself or through a discount reseller like Expedia.com. So it should go without saying that if you've scored a bargain basement rate for your hotel room, you'll most likely be placed in the smallest room with a close-up view of a brick wall. This may seem unfair, but in New York City you get what you pay for.

№ 501

GETTING THE BEST RATE

"You need a cozy, decadent cocoon."

Hotel rooms in NYC are among the most expensive in the Western world, with a pronounced lack of budget boutique hotels easily found in cities like Paris. A decent room under $200/night is something of a rarity, but with prices fluctuating according to demand like airline tickets, the same room that costs $450 one day might go down to $195 on another. If you're feeling the need to be frugal, take pride, as many a savvy NY lady does, in being able to get the most for your hard-earned dollars without sacrificing style, a good location, and most of all, safety. A lady doesn't have to slum it if she's careful to plan in advance and keep her ear to the ground. Always check the hotel's own website first (especially if they have a guarantee on lowest price), but don't neglect to search on engines that notify you when rooms become available within your budget (such as Priceline.com). When comparing hotel rates, don't forget to factor in added costs of WiFi access and breakfast if not included, and the hefty State, City and Hotel Occupancy taxes. And since you can get a toasted bagel with cream cheese and a hot coffee at any deli for under $5, reconsider the pricey hotel breakfast. Unless of course you want it served in bed.

▟▙▟▙

Remember

All hotel rooms are subject to a NY State tax of 4%, NY City sales tax of 8.875% , Hotel Room Occupancy tax of $2+5.875%, and an additional fee of $1.50. More simply, you'll be charged 14.75% plus $3.50 per day in taxes, in addition to the advertised rate.

A Note for Solo Adventurers

For ladies tackling Manhattan on their own, it's best to choose accommodations that are central. One with its own restaurant can provide a great stand-by dining option when you don't want to venture far after dark, and solo females may feel more comfortable at the hotel bar enjoying a glass of wine rather than braving a random bar on the Lower East Side. Forget about scrimping pennies on this trip. You're here to awaken your sensuality and embrace your sexiness, which can't be done if you have bed bugs or moldy bathrooms. You need a cozy, decadent cocoon. A place to prepare the psyche – as well as the body – for another day or night on the town. A place where you wake up feeling like a true New Yorker. Get to know the staff, tip well (and in person), and don't hesitate to make the room your home away from home with flowers, an inspirational framed photo or two, and perhaps your own favorite scent (careful with the candles, they may be a no-no).

WHAT TO PACK

"New Yorkers won't bat an eyelash whether you're in a ballgown or a track suit."

Solo Getaways

- When choosing your clothes, try channeling the feminine, yet no-nonsense style of Lauren Bacall: tailored pants with a cowl-neck sweater or crisp white shirt and a bright scarf. Above all, your travel wardrobe should be chic, yet comfortable and — most important – mobile. You don't want to be slowed down by fussy ensembles or unreasonable shoes. Save the micro minis and macro-cleavage for the Bahamas. When you're solo, the sexiest thing in your wardrobe should be your attitude.

- An eyeshade and ear plugs for sleeping in late.

- Calling cards. Bonus points if you've had them made especially for your trip. Much more elegant than scribbling your e-mail on a wine coaster.

- A stylish hat for bad hair days. Good ones form a triple barrier to the sun, rain, and chilly air.

- If you don't have anything to wear, pack an empty suitcase and a built-in excuse to shop.

Gentleman Callers?

Perhaps you don't plan on staying solo very long. In that case, there's no need to be sneaky about bringing your new Manhattan beau back to your room (as long as it's not a single). The unwritten rule regarding discretion – both yours and the hotel staff's – will be respected. Just don't give them reason to think you're "working" – a lady doesn't have a revolving door into her bedroom. And don't forget to hang the "Do not Disturb" sign on the door.

A Trip with the Gals

- You can dress more fun and flirty when you're traveling with the pack. There's a certain amount of safety in numbers, as Carrie and the SATC ladies demonstrated. And hopefully your best friend will let you know when the hem of your skirt is tucked into your waistband.

- Essential: fabulous shoes and at least one slinky dress.

- Extra hangers and a spare hair dryer or two.

- Sexy short-shorts if you plan on joining a pole-dancing class.

A Note on In-Room Parties

While the creative minibar selection has come a long way in the past few years, it may be more economical to discreetly bring your own inaugural bottle of bubbly (this is when those hotel ice buckets come in handy). Just try to keep the feasting to a minimum and remember the cleaning staff are your friends; don't leave food trash strewn around or stuffed into the tiny waste basket, take it out yourself. Ladies' voices tend to carry, so be respectful of your neighbors, especially those couples trying to get into the mood, and take the raucous party down to the hotel bar where you're liveliness – and gratuities – will be welcomed.

For You and Your Man

- New Yorkers won't bat an eyelash whether you're in a ballgown or a track suit, so let this be your chance to wear all those fancy outfits you never have the occasion to wear back home.

- All of those fabulous stilettos you can only wear when you have a man's arm to steady you (preferably a man who knows how to hail a cab).

- Nothing but the most exquisite lingerie you own. Don't have any? Then bring none and exclaim once checked into your hotel room, "Oh my! I totally forgot to pack panties!" After he's completed a thorough strip search to verify this fact, lead him (and his Platinum card) to the nearest lingerie boutique (see the Sexy You chapter for addresses).

- If you've gone the "sexy slumming" route of budget accommodations, bring some scented bath oils to erase any unpleasant aromas that may be lingering.

- Extra scarves: use them to throw over any overly-bright lights in your hotel room, or to tie your naughty playmate to the bed (bonus: scarves don't show up in airport x-ray machines like handcuffs do).

- Many rooms are equipped with an iPod docking station, so bring along a custom mix of sexy music for instant ambience (and to drown out any distracting sounds coming from adjacent rooms).

SOHO SANCTUARY

Spa, Beauty and Fitness for Women

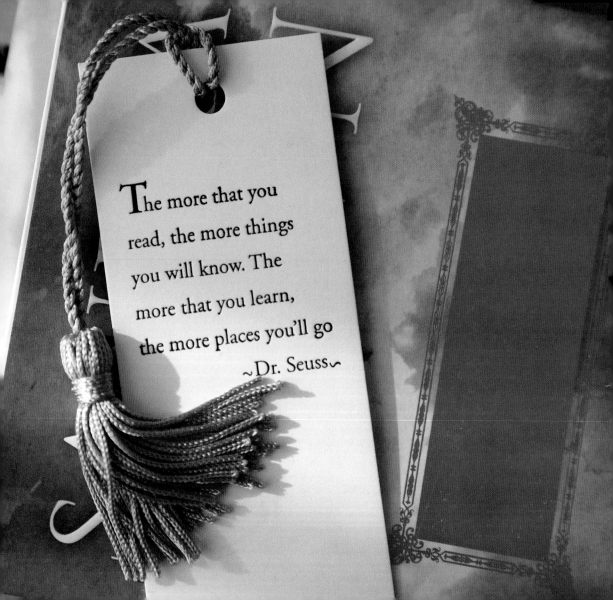

The more that you read, the more things you will know. The more that you learn, the more places you'll go

~Dr. Seuss~

HOTELS

MANDARIN ORIENTAL

80 COLUMBUS CIRCLE AT 60TH STREET
NYC 10023
212 805 8800
COLUMBUS CIRCLE STATION
WWW.MANDARINORIENTAL.COM/NEWYORK/

In your New York fantasies, you always see yourself strolling in Central Park on a gorgeous day, a pretty dress, lunch by the lake, perhaps a handsome gentleman at your side, the background of historic skyscrapers, the sound of the horse drawn carriages, the languid pace of the fairytale city. And after the sun sets you'll simply cross Columbus Circle to your hotel in the sky, where even the lobby is on the 35th floor, far from the rush of pedestrians. And a bonus, the city's finest shopping mall, small yet chic, at your feet complete with a trendy bakery and Whole Foods for picnic supplies. Even rooms without a view are the height of luxury, decorated with an Asian touch. Spoil yourself in the restaurant, the bar, or the wonderfully plush spa, enjoying the hotel's discreet yet world-renowned service. From $990.

FOUR SEASONS
57 EAST 57TH STREET
212 758 5700
59TH STREET/LEXINGTON STATION
WWW.FOURSEASONS.COM/NEWYORKFS

Possibly the best curb appeal in Manhattan, the impressive Four Seasons won't leave any doubt that you're a VIP. You have arrived. Enter its vast museum-like lobby, check in to the largest rooms in town, and feel the classic NY vibe of its sober, minimalist decor of caramel and neutral tones, clean lines, right out of a Frank Sinatra film or an episode of Mad Men. The show is outside the windows, with nothing to interrupt the views. Let your man get his Big on; don't forget the bow tie and pour me a Scotch on the rocks, sweetheart. Your walk-in closets will have you shopping at the nearby Madison Avenue boutiques to fill the void. From $855.

GRAMMERCY PARK

2 LEXINGTON AVENUE
212 920 3300
23RD STREET/LEXINGTON STATION
WWW.GRAMERCYPARKHOTEL.COM

If you have a flair for the theatrical and are looking for
the right stage to shine in all your feminine sexiness,
Ian Schrager's moody decor certainly fits the bill.
Dark, brooding, sensual, seductive...the rooms alone
are enough to bring out your feminine wiles with your
helpless Romeo, but the bonus icing on the cake is that
you'll be able to saunter right into one of the hottest
bars in town, the hotel's own Rose Bar and Jade Bar,
with a wink to the concierge who will make sure
the Lady doesn't get the ugly end of the velvet rope
treatment. From $600.

CROSBY STREET

270 LAFAYETTE STREET
212 226 6400
PRINCE STREET STATION
WWW.FIRMDALE.COM

If you don't immediately want to move here
permanently, leave your Lady credentials at the door
and have your estrogen levels checked. Fabulously
feminine without being frivolous, the Crosby
combines bold florals, exotic antiques, a solid influence
from mother nature in natural textures and the
masculine balance of solid oversized furnishings. Its
immense loft-style windows give it a historic SoHo
vibe but this custom-built property opened in late
2009 is simply adept at blending magnificently in
with the surroundings. Enjoy little luxuries like the
Champagne-only minibar and bespoke "Le Jardin
10012" scented bath products by Miller Harris
guilt-free: Crosby Street is one of the first hotels in
the city to be certified by the U.S. Green Building
Council. Mingle at the bar and restaurant, or avoid
the paparazzi certainly trailing your every move in the
guests-only private garden courtyard. From $495.

60 THOMPSON

60 THOMPSON STREET
212 431 0400
SPRING STREET STATION
WWW.THOMPSONHOTELS.COM

You love the edgy vibe of SoHo but still want the sleek and stylish atmosphere of a contemporary hotel like the Thompson 60. Rooms have a clean, modern design with dark wood and leather accents, marble bathrooms and Kiehl's bath products. The duplex loft is ideal for honeymooners or a group of friends looking to enjoy extraordinary views and plenty of space to spread out. You can mingle with discerning locals in the Kittichai Thai restaurant or seductive Thom Bar, but only guests have the privilege of access to the exotic Moroccan-style A60 rooftop lounge with stunning views over Manhattan. You're not in Midtown, but you're hardly slumming it, darling. From $400.

GANSEVOORT

18 9TH AVENUE
212 206 6700
8TH AVENUE/14TH STREET STATION
WWW.HOTELGANSEVOORT.COM

SOHO GRAND

310 WEST BROADWAY
212 965 3000
CANAL STREET STATION
WWW.SOHOGRAND.COM

A resort in the Meatpacking district? And why not? If that means an oasis of pampering, style, and fun in one of the hottest districts in Manhattan, then the Gansevoort delivers an impressive punch. You and the ladies will find plenty of closet space, a pool to frolic and pose in bikinis, and a rooftop bar to celebrate the day's (or evening's) exploits. See and be seen with a young and hip artsy entrepreneurial crowd. If you want the same resort amenities and edgy feel in Midtown, check out their newly-opened **Gansevoort Park Avenue Resort** (420 Park Avenue South, New York 10016, www.gansevoortpark. com, 212 317 2901). From $400.

Located on the south end of SoHo just off the gritty Canal Street, this stylish boutique hotel pays homage to Gotham with its masculine vibe and dramatic neo-industrial lobby. Rooms are luxurious if small, with Frette linens, clawfoot tubs for two, and excellent views over SoHo and the Manhattan skyline (reserve a room on one of the upper floors). If you desire more space, the 1970s SoHo Loft inspired suites feature vintage furnishings and huge terraces. Note: Make sure you tell your taxi driver it's on WEST Broadway. From $350.

THE BOWERY

335 BOWERY
212 505 9100
BLEEKER STREET/LEXINGTON STATION
WWW.THEBOWERYHOTEL.COM

Sometimes even a lady likes a bit of rough. The
Bowery district is one of the few neighborhoods left in
Manhattan where a little street sense goes a long way,
although today there are as many luxury townhouses and
organic food shops as pawn shops and loitering down-
on-their-luck locals. The historic music halls are gone
and the legendary CBGB closed in 2006, but avant garde
design shops and up-and-coming designer boutiques
have happily filled the gap. The lobby is all dark wood
paneling, cozy fireplace in winter, leather chesterfields
and overstuffed armchairs; you'll feel like settling in for
a snifter of Cognac. Upstairs, the rooms are sober, chic,
in Pre-war NY style perfect for those seeking an Old
Money atmosphere. Shabby chic with crisp white linens,
colonial-style ceiling fans and dark wood antiques, and
all of the modern amenities discreetly tucked away. The
floor-to-ceiling windows offer nostalgic views of, yes,
tenement buildings. The hot tub terrace may be just
what you need to soothe your aching muscles after a
night on the town. From $325.

MUSE

130 WEST 46TH STREET
212 485 2400
49TH STREET STATION
WWW.THEMUSEHOTEL.COM

Nothing can get you in a New York state of mind faster
than the bright lights and bustling crowds of Times
Square and Broadway. But just because you like the
campy glitz of it all doesn't mean you have to settle on a
tacky tourist trap hotel. The Muse is an oasis of chic and
comfort in the heart of the action. Guests can socialize
in the sexy low-lit lobby bar with complimentary wine
during happy hour, or hide out in the stylish Art Deco
inspired rooms, where you and your lover will find
it hard to extract yourselves from the blissfully cozy
beds. And if your luggage got lost somewhere over the
Atlantic, you'll find racy pajamas and a few naughty
accessories available from the room service catalog.
From $295.

THE STANDARD

848 WASHINGTON STREET & W 13TH ST
212 645 4646
8TH AVENUE/14TH STREET STATION
WWW.STANDARDHOTELS.COM

Bring out your playful streak in this 1960s-style kitsch
centerpiece of the gentrified Meatpacking district.
The perpetually Ray Ban clad clientele and Clockwork
Orange-meets-The Love Boat decor might imply
the Standard is more about cool than comfort, but
how could anyone resist the naughty possibilities of
bathrooms with transparent glass walls? Just remember
to draw the curtains, as flashing the families strolling
on the converted rail-to-trail walkway outside is *so*
unoriginal. Save the see-and-be-seen exhibitionism for
the hotel's newly-opened rooftop bar, Le Bain, with
oversized Jacuzzi, pink waterbed loungers, and ultra-
kitsch synthetic grass. From $295.

GRACE

125 WEST 45TH STREET
212 380 2700
47-50TH STREET/ROCKEFELLER STATION
WWW.ROOM-MATEHOTELS.COM

Perhaps you're one of those lucky ladies whose most flattering accessory is a swimming pool. And at this bright and cheerful hotel just off Times Square, it's all about the pool. Show off your graceful backstroke in the heated water, lounge with a cocktail from the poolside bar, or sooth stiletto-weary feet in the steam room, you're sure to have an appreciative audience. Ikea-esque rooms are barely big enough to hold much more than your bikini and a tube of lipstick, but the empty mini-fridges are perfect for stocking up on your own bubbly and snacks. Note: No need to be a guest to enjoy the pool's theme parties and Happy Hour drink specials. From $215.

STAY

157 WEST 47TH STREET
212 768 3700
49TH STREET STATION
WWW.STAYHOTELNY.COM

Manhattan ladies know how to make the most out of what they've got. The Stay will get you the street cred and the style of a trendy boutique hotel without the sky high prices. Not that cool comes cheap, but here you pay for the location, the fashion attitude, and the easy access to the hip Aspen Club Bar just off the lobby. Rooms are for sleeping, in minimalist white (and minimal space) with walk-in showers and fashion prints on the walls. From $200.

NIGHT

132 WEST 45TH STREET
212 835 9600
47-50TH STREET/ROCKEFELLER STATION
WWW.NIGHTHOTELNY.COM

Vamp is still your favorite nail color, you wear black
boots in summer, and you like your music loud. The
sexiest of the Vikram Chatwal hotels will appeal to your
inner Joan Jett with its very contemporary black and
white take on Goth decor. Aside from the penthouse
with its round bed and terrace view of nothing, rooms
are for ladies who travel light yet appreciate Frette
linens and down comforters. You can strike a pose in
the night-club-styled lobby bar, where you'll have plenty
of room to stretch out those lovely legs. From $250.

Note

Some of the hottest bars in Manhattan are found
in the city's sexy hotels, often with excellent
rooftop views of the skyline. Check out our
recommendations in the After Dark chapter.

ACE

20 W 29TH STREET
212 679 2222
28TH STREET STATION
WWW.ACEHOTEL.COM

Whether you're in the mood to play the role of aspiring indie rocker or adoring groupie, you can indulge your fantasies at this edgy new hotel in the Flatiron district's historic Tin Pan Alley. Argue over who looks sexiest in the boxer-style hooded robes, giggle at the colorful kitsch Japanese products in the roadie case style minibar, or spin a few LPs on the in-room turntable. Some rooms are even thoughtfully equipped with a guitar in case inspiration calls for an impromptu jam session or a sexy serenade. More than just a hotel, Ace is a universe unto itself with two trendy fashion boutiques, a bustling coffee shop, an old school Manhattan restaurant, a basement bar and boxing room, and a huge lobby lounge and bar that mixes contemporary artworks with the original turn-of-the-(last) century architectural details such as mosaic tiled floors and high molded ceilings. The stylish yet unpretentious atmosphere makes it a popular hangout throughout the day for an eclectic crowd of students, local businessmen and fashion industry types. Single ladies should schedule accordingly for the prime cruising time during happy hour. No backstage pass needed. From $225.

HUDSON

356 WEST 58TH STREET
212 554 6000
59TH STREET/COLUMBUS CIRCLE STATION
WWW.HUDSONHOTEL.COM

Can't imagine wasting a moment of your time cooped up in a hotel room? At the Hudson, the tiny, wood-paneled boat-cabin style rooms are perfect for dropping off your shopping bags from next door's Columbus Circle, for changing into a sexy sundress for a stroll in nearby Central Park, or for catching a quick catnap before checking out the talent at the hotel's chic Library Bar or trendy Hudson Bar. And if the combination of old Manhattan brick and Philippe Starck Plexiglas doesn't get you in the mood, try the leafy sanctuary of the private Sky Terrace in season. For couples, consider splurging on the loft for more legroom and river views. From $200.

GERSHWIN

7 EAST 27TH STREET
212 545 8000
28TH STREET STATION
WWW.GERSHWINHOTEL.COM

Bohemian babes on a budget will feel right at home in this vintage artsy hotel with the unforgettable façade. Like the clientele, rooms are eclectic, some a tad scruffy around the edges. But the price is right whether you go for the bunk beds on 2nd, the Fabulosa 4th floor (for up-and-coming-models) or opt for the relatively luxurious Cozy Canadian Cocoon, complete with a moose head over the bed. Artworks are displayed on every available surface, from the theatrical lobby to the well-stocked reading room and the health-conscious coffee bar. All perfectly innocent reasons for choosing to stay at the Gershwin, despite its suspiciously convenient location between the Museum of Sex and La Trapèze Adults Club. From $110.

"There was always something immensely comic to her in the thought of living elsewhere than New York. She could not regard as serious proposals that she share a western residence."

—DOROTHY PARKER, FROM BIG BLONDE

A ROOM OF ONE'S OWN
Apartment Rentals

"Don't call me a saint — I don't want to be dismissed that easily." —DOROTHY DAY

Some travelers adore the luxury hotel experience of 24/7 room service and the personal attention of attentive staff. But there are also benefits to renting your own apartment in Manhattan. There's privacy and discretion, the feeling of enjoying the city like a local, and the luxury of cooking in one's own kitchen. And often the price of an apartment rental is far lower than a hotel room, perfect if you're on a budget or looking for a space big enough for a group of friends. Caveat emptor is de rigueur when renting a private apartment. It may be a pinch more expensive, but we recommend you use the services of a reputable booking agency to avoid any surprises.

A I R B N B is an online marketplace where owners or agencies can advertise properties. Booking and payments are made through the site (which also provides customer support), and each property shows ratings by former guests. www.airbnb.com

M E T R O - H O M E is a NY-based agency in business for over 20 years. They have basic properties from studios to 2-bedrooms in the Financial District, Greenwich Village, Chelsea, Midtown, Times Square and Murray Hill. Many properties have access to a fitness center, lounge and laundry. www.metro-home.com

N E W Y O R K H A B I T A T originally opened in 1989 and has since grown to include over 10,000 apartments in its database, including B&Bs. They charge a small fee to put travelers in direct contact with owners. There are a few luxury properties, and prices are competitive. www.nyhabitat.com

A K A is an aparthotel, or hotel with fully-equipped kitchens and on-site fitness center and café, as well as serviced apartments, for those who want something between a hotel and an apartment. Locations include Times Square, Sutton Place, United Nations, and Central Park. Rates are reasonable. www.hotelaka.com

M A N H A T T A N G E T A W A Y S owner Judith Glynn maintains a beautifully kept and managed network of bed-and-breakfast rooms (from $110 nightly) and un-hosted apartments (from $150) around the city. There's a 3-night minimum stay, and credit cards are accepted. www.manhattangetaways.com.

PART III

Sexy You

Known as the melting pot, New York City is a mélange of different styles, colors, attitudes, sizes, and backgrounds. Come what you are and as you may – that's where the real beauty lies here. Though Carrie Bradshaw's years of tottering on Manolos and chasing unsuitable men have influenced many visitors' own quest for beauty in the Big Apple, this manufactured high ideal is hardly the real bite. As the center for advertising and media, New York City forever feels like the U.N. of beauty, making peace with more than one ideal and always pushing the envelope on what's attractive and appealing – good news for any visitor.

Gorgeous, sexy, stylish, and successful women are as easy to come by as taxi cabs in Manhattan. This city is chock full of über models and actresses doing everything they can to look the part and make it big, but sometimes the most breathtaking women are the ones wearing flip flops and whisking their bags of Trader Joe's groceries through Union Square. New York cinema icons such as Gena Rowlands in *Gloria* and Diane Keaton in *Annie Hall* say more about the true allure of Manhattan's women than any "stick figure with no soul".

Shopping the Big Apple

Though haute couture has its place here, locals have a way of mixing it up. Combining the high with the low, Madison Avenue with the Bowery, vintage and new, cheap and expensive, ugly and beautiful – style is less a matter of taste than it is about creativity. It takes a certain amount of artistry to balance fine pieces from Barney's with items procured from a second-hand store or found in the back of a closet. Expect plenty of black – clichés are clichés for a reason – the color that never goes out of style also has the power to make anyone look ten pounds lighter. Whatever your style, there's likely to be a neighborhood to match it that's just a short subway ride away—from the tailored and tony Upper East Side down to the hip and edgy East Village or the lively and trendy Meatpacking District.

IN A NEW YORK MINUTE

"I'm not interested in age. People who tell me their age are silly. You're as old as you feel." —ELIZABETH ARDEN

One part classy bird and one part sexy street warrior, a New York woman is unapologetically put together and confident enough to push her way through evening subway rush hour without even scuffing up her butter-soft Italian boots. Unlike their L.A. West Coast sisters with salt swept hair, Gotham's local ladies actually look like they make a colossal effort in the morning. After the primping, preening, and cleverly put together outfit, comes the right accessories: sunglasses, tasteful and delicate jewelry, a fabulous handbag roomy enough to fit a little dog, a "skinny" designer latte to go, and of course, an iPhone. Caffeine, UV protection, and constant communication – now that's a native.

Battle of the Beauty Queens

A century ago, two immigrants moved to Manhattan to open cosmetic boutiques. Through hard work and sharp business acumen, Elizabeth Arden and Helena Rubinstein soon became two of the most successful women entrepreneurs in the world, creating what is today the $150 billion global health and beauty industry. Part of their success has been attributed to their fierce competitiveness as they constantly tried to outdo each other with newer and better products. In the 50 years that the two women lived and worked in Manhattan — just a few blocks apart! — they made it a point to never meet in person.

"Coming as I did from a conservative European background, my attitude as an individualist — a girl who preferred to make it on her own rather than stay at home — was all the more unusual."

— HELENA RUBINSTEIN

Spas

There's plenty of action and energy in the city, sometimes so much it seems palpable…and sometimes it is. That's why the beauticians of this gritty city stay constantly busy. Gotham's glamazons don't let the filth get under their skin, instead they arm themselves with expert hands and sublime treatments to ease out stress and grime from their hard working and hard playing bodies. In a city where everyone is wrapped in armor, a spa experience is the chance to let it all hang out. Solo, with friends, or a sexy date, spa-goers emerge refreshed, rejuvenated, and replenished — ready once again to face the frenetic energy with clean and impeccably moisturized skin.

Caudalíe Vinothérapie Spa

AT THE PLAZA HOTEL
ONE WEST 58TH ST, 4TH FLOOR
212 265 3182
COLUMBUS CIRCLE/57TH ST STATION
WWW.CAUDALIE-USA.COM

Housed in one of New York's most celebrated hotels, this sleek spa is a great spot for a good rubdown with your girlfriends. Grapes from Bordeaux's Chateau Haut Lafitte transform wine into divine treatments. Scrubs, wraps, and soaks, like the sumptuous red Vine Barrel Bath and Honey and Wine Wrap start at around $75. After the intoxication, there's a glass of the real thing waiting for you in the wine lounge.

Haven

150 MERCER ST
212 343 3515
PRINCE ST STATION
WWW.HAVENSOHO.COM

Nestled amid world-class shopping on cobblestoned mercer Street, Haven appears slightly underdressed for its Soho environs. Still, this below-the-radar spot is a fave with celebs looking for a low profile spiff-up. Perfect manicures and pedicures include organic nail polish and scrubs, from $35 to $70. Their thorough facials leave you with pores fully evacuated, skin analyzed, smoothed and soothed, from $110.

Mandarin Oriental

80 COLUMBUS CIRCLE 35TH FL.
212 805 8880
COLUMBUS CIRCLE/57TH ST STATION
WWW.MANDARINORIENTAL.COM/NEWYORK/SPA

East-meets-West on the 35th and 36th floors. Soak in tubs, swim laps, and breathe easier amid sweeping views of Central Park and the Hudson River. Treatments start at $450 and use elements of traditional Chinese medicine. The three-hour Time Ritual in the VIP Suite for two, $1,500, is pampering perfection with side-by-side massages. After, slip into the private elevated bath and steam room. Then get cozy by the fireplace and share a bento box with your honey.

Red Door Spa

691 FIFTH AVE
212 546 0200
5TH AVE/53RD ST STATION
WWW.REDDOORSPAS.COM

Local ladies know the entrance to heaven: the red doors on 5th avenue. This flagship spa has been frequented by the city's uptown socialites for over 25 years. Despite a somewhat clinical feel, the specially-tailored facials for $120 are worth a trip to midtown. Once a week, a doctor brings in something stronger than lactic acid to restore vitality with lunchtime appointments for Botox, Juvederm, or Restylane.

SOHO SANCTUARY

119 MERCER ST, 3RD FLOOR
212 334 5550
PRINCE ST STATION
WWW.SOHOSANCTUARY.COM

This veritable sanctuary is hidden in an otherwise inconspicuous building. Deluxe nail care with extra long massage time and two intensive masks start at $70. With the spa's lovely lavender-infused steam room and candlelit lounge area, an appointment for an hour-long massage—from hot stone to Thai Yoga—will have you lingering much longer. Fitness and Pilates are also available.

FRESH

57 SPRING STREET
212 925 0099
SPRING ST STATION
WWW.FRESH.COM

Fresh is constantly on the "best of" lists in magazines like Allure and InStyle. At this Soho spot you'll find yummy Brown Sugar Body Polish, soy-based creams and cleansers, and perfect sheer lip colors with SPF 15. All triple-milled soaps—in exotic scents like mangosteen, coriander-lavender, violet-moss—come wrapped in the prettiest paper, for around $14 each.

GREAT JONES SPA

29 GREAT JONES ST
212 505 3185
BLEECKER ST STATION
WWW.GREATJONESSPA.COM

Equipped with a plunge pool, thermal hot tub, chakra-light steam room, river-rock sauna, three-story waterfall, and a skylit lounge, this spa will turn any tough city girl into a delicate flower. experience world-class treatments from turkey, Japan and Russia; the five-step red Flower Hammam massage uses natural beautifiers like Moroccan mint tea and silt, olive stones, coffee, and amber. From $50.

Russian & Turkish Baths

268 EAST 10TH ST
212 674 9250
ASTOR PLACE STATION
WWW.RUSSIANTURKISHBATHS.COM

This east Village landmark (circa 1832) may lack elegance, but locals love the $30 admission for access to the saunas, steam rooms, and cold dunk pool. Get kneaded like perogie dough for an hour, $90, or whacked and exfoliated with oak leaves for $35. After detox, there's beer and borscht to feel "strong like bull". Open to women Wednesdays 2-10pm; towels, robes, and slippers included.

Cosmetics & Perfume

Nothing signals the arrival of a beautiful woman like the scent of expensive, fine perfume as she breezes past tables in a restaurant. A touch of burgundy on the lips and smudged on the edge of a martini glass speaks volumes in a crowded bar. Lush, thick, dark lashes shield sultry eyes from the city's harsh elements. Never overly wrought, the painted New York lady chooses one feature and gives it the spotlight – and a little color.

Low Fat, Thigh High

Cottage cheese. Orange peel. Hail damage. Call it what you like, cellulite is anything but pretty. A little jiggle shouldn't prevent you from slipping into that hip hugging dress, since plenty of spas offer treatments to get you smoothed and toned. At Aqua Beauty Bar (on 14th Street, a block west of Union Square), the Celluless Method uses ultrasound and noninvasive therapies, which work on all stages of cellulite, by breaking down the nasty stuff to encourage lymphatic drainage. Bliss Spa, the perennial Soho favorite, has an entire line of products, known as Fatgirlslim, which can help smooth things out. Using grapefruit essential oil, a seaweed mask and a heated wrap along with dry brushing to stimulate circulation, countless ladies leave ready to hit the city's best boutiques and—shudder!—even a lingerie shop.

AEDES DE VENUSTAS

9 CHRISTOPHER ST
212 206 8675
CHRISTOPHER ST STATION
WWW.AEDES.COM

This 15-year-old shop on Christopher Street is like visiting Gypsy Rose Lee's boudoir. Latin for "Temple of Beauty," this store greets visitors with a crystal chandelier, sexy red walls, taxidermy peacocks, and fifty different brands of French, Italian, and American fine and rare perfumes –brands like Kilian, Serge Lutens, and French fragrance house L'Artisan Parfumeur – starting at $150 a bottle.

KIEHL'S SINCE 1851

109 THIRD AVE
212 677 3171
IRVING PLACE STATION
WWW.KIEHLS.COM

Purveyors of au naturale skin and hair care products since 1851, the original "pharmacy" still stands as the flagship East Village shop. Today, this popular spot has perennial favorites like their facial moisturizer next to innovative new products. Though Kiehl's has countless stores worldwide, this shop is the only one where you can purchase first run exclusive items like the vintage-inspired Kiehl's razor.

BOND NO. 9

9 BOND ST
212 228 1732
BLEEKER ST STATION
WWW.BONDNO9.COM

This one-of-kind perfumerie stocks 40 fragrances inspired by the city's fabled neighborhoods. There's the zingy zest of "Little Italy" and the spicy, and high-powered notes of "Wall Street". At this flagship shop, choose a vintage atomizer, starting at $80, and fill it with your choice of scent for about $40 an ounce. The shop also hosts scent parties where you can mix your own perfume.

The Cosmetics Counter

The city is chock full of generic super-chain Sephoras but for a more classic cosmetic shopping experience, head to one of the fine department stores. Henri Bendel's puts the fun back into cosmetic shopping with some of the most cutting-edge collections like M.A.C., Nars, Trish McEvoy, Laura Mercier, Mally Beauty, Dr. Brandt, and Freeze 24/7 – many of these lines were originally launched at the store – plus make-up brushes and tools fit for a professional. Bloomingdales is the place to stock up on the high-quality basics like Lancôme, Clinique, and Bobbi Brown. Saks Fifth Avenue's beautiful marble-covered grand hall will provide the most memorable scent-shopping experience with its sizable collections of brands like NARS, Mac, T. LeClerc, La Mer, and Chanel.

Hair & Nails

Strong nails and soft hair go far in this town. Long and glossy, curly and loose, asymmetrically intriguing, or short and pixie-ish—anything works as long as it is well-suited to the wearer and says "unfussy, yet super stylish." Complete a flawless and not-too-ostentatious look with perfect brows, well-groomed hair-down-there, and nails that are tough enough to handle morning rush hour in Times Square. And don't forget the "mani/pedi" -- the term of endearment for the beloved activity of unwinding at a neighborhood nail salon. It's not rare to see a woman during the city's legendary frigid winters dashing across the street in a heavy overcoat with flip-flops, so as not to ruin her freshly painted toes.

"Beauty is only skin deep, but ugly goes clean to the bone." —Dorothy Parker

EVA SCRIVO

50 BOND STREET
212 677 7315
BLEECKER ST STATION
WWW.EVASCRIVO.COM

Beloved beauty expert Eva Scrivo's downtown salon is
frequented by celebs and locals alike. Antique chandeliers,
polished wood floors, and high ceilings set the stage for
artfully cut hair. All stylists are trained in the Uncut technique, Scrivo's trademark style that utilizes both scissors
and razor on both wet and dry hair to create lines that fall
naturally, preventing the common awkwardness of "just
cut" styles. Cuts are $90 to $350, depending on the stylist.

BEEHIVE HAIR SALON

115 NORTH 7TH ST
7187 82 8376
BROOKLYN, BEDFORD AVE STATION
WWW.THEBEEHIVESALONBROOKLYN.COM

Located in Brooklyn's popular "Billyburg" district, this
fun, quirky salon is the best place to go for affordable
rockstar hair. Willing to work with any hair type, the
amiable stylists listen patiently to their clients and can
deliver both classic cuts as well as the asymmetrical,
super stylish looks that fill the local bars. Best of all,
prices won't bleed into your Champagne budget since
cuts start at $40.

RED MARKET

32 GANSEVOORT ST
212 929 9600
8TH AVE/14TH ST STATION
WWW.REDMARKETNYC.COM

This hair salon gives stylish cuts late at night in a funky,
industrial setting when the rest of the Meatpacking
District neighborhood gets busy downing cocktails.
Pegged the best late night salon by *New York Magazine*,
Red Market provides high style hair by two Frederic
Fekkai alums. Cuts and color treatments start at $100
and include a complimentary glass of wine. On Saturday
nights, a local dj keeps the hair party hopping.

DEVACHAN

560 BROADWAY, LOWER LEVEL
212 274 8686
PRINCE ST STATION
WWW.DEVACHANSALON.COM

Curly girls have no fear! These pioneers have unique and
effective techniques to transform every frizzy-headed
lady into a corkscrew goddess. With the Devacut, hair
gets chopped dry, curl-by-curl, while in the Pintura
color technique, curls get painted individually for an
eye-popping look. The salon's own products keep up
the spring, like a non-shampoo cleanser and a lavender-
scented refreshing mist. Cuts start at $100.

BUMBLE & BUMBLE

415 WEST 13TH ST, 8TH FLOOR
212 521 6500
8TH AVE/14TH ST STATION
WWW.BUMBLEANDBUMBLE.COM

In the six-floor, world-famous House of Bumble amazing things happen. The Bumble hair movement started in the 1970s, but cuts live in present and future tense. Famous for its editorial work and Fashion Week styling, this salon has transformed many fashion and acting careers. If you have to wait your turn to turn some heads, head upstairs to the lounge for a cup of tea and a little treat. From $90 to $250.

PIERRE MICHEL SALON

135 EAST 57TH ST
212 755-9500
59TH ST/LEXINGTON STATION
WWW.PIERREMICHELBEAUTY.COM

Forget mascara—it's gloopy, flaky, and in rainy city weather may very well run down your cheeks. Instead head to Pierre Michel Salon for luxurious eyelash extensions from $350 and up. These lovely lashes are made from a silk material and attached, in a two-hour procedure, by a specially formulated adhesive. The overall look is surprisingly natural and very lush. You'll look sexy and wide-eyed the moment you wake up in the morning and look your man directly in his eyes.

RESCUE BEAUTY LOUNGE

34 GANSEVOORT STREET, 2ND FLOOR
212 206 6409
8TH AVE/14TH ST STATION
WWW.RESCUEBEAUTY.COM

Tucked away in the hip Meatpacking District, this posh salon keeps the business of beautifying hands and feet super clean with gorgeous white, ethereal décor. Consider a Recovery Manicure, $40, to treat ragged cuticles and hangnails, or a restorative Oxygen Therapy to show off naked nails for $25. And for color, the Rescue nail polishes lack formaldehyde and other common lacquer nasties.

COMPLETELY BARE

25 BOND STREET
BLEECKER ST STATION
212 3666 060
WWW.COMPLETELYBARE.COM

After a breakup, Jennifer Love Hewitt had a good friend vagazzle her "precious lady" so it "shined like a disco ball." At this downtown spa, any woman can get "completely bare with flair" and make her bedroom partner see stars. The spa uses special ouchless wax and Swarovski crystals to decorate, from $115. Sparkles last around five days. For extra-sensitive ladies, try the Relax Wax with numbing cream.

Shobha NYC

594 BROADWAY
212 931 8363
BROADWAY/LAFAYETTE ST STATION
WWW.MYSHOBHA.COM

Ohm Spa

260 5TH AVE, 7TH FLOOR
212 481 7892
28TH ST STATION
WWW.OHMSPA.COM

Perfect brows are as imperative to a New York City gal's look as a great handbag, and no one shapes brows better than Shobha NYC with hair threading. This ancient technique dates back centuries in Arabia and South Asia, and provides both precision and near-ouchless eyebrow beautification, starting at $20. Don't be daunted by the fierce ladies who keep one end of the thread in the mouth and seamlessly –almost magically – wrap the other end around strays, whipping them into submission to give you a flawless, unforgettably arched look.

For something above and beyond the city's quick nail fix, Ohm Spa delivers specialty mani/pedis like the green tea antioxidant and spa ritual treatments, which include eco-friendly and vegan products and aromatherapy paraffin, starting at $75. Add extra massage time for tired tootsies and legs – 15 minutes for $25 – and you'll be ready to pound the pavement again.

Beauty on a Budget

For ladies on a tight budget, the city has plenty of places for a quick beauty fix. Convenient and inexpensive nail and waxing salons pepper nearly every single street. A quick mani/pedi – usually $12 to $25 – and cheap bikini wax for around $20 are within anyone's reach. Use caution—some spots are cleaner than others. The best bet is to head to more residential neighborhood where the salons have a loyal, regular customer base. Good neighborhoods include the Upper West and East Side, the West Village, Soho, and in Brooklyn, Park Slope or Brooklyn Heights.

Body Art

Badass New Yorkers do two things: wear ironic t-shirts and get awesome tattoos. The best of edgy or beautiful art can adorn your ankle, hip, or shoulder. It's a memorable surprise for whoever undresses you, and the perfect souvenir to take home that says you'll love New York forever.

NY ADORNED

47 SECOND AVE
212 473 0007
2ND AVE/LOWER EAST SIDE STATION
WWW.NYADORNED.COM

From the exterior, NY Adorned looks like a cute little jewelry shop. Burnt sienna-colored walls and a gorgeous, dripping chandelier make you think this might be a good place to procure an engagement ring. That is, until you hear the familiar buzzing in the back and see customers furiously examining the dozens of look books for their own unforgettable tattoo. Piercings of gold and silver with precious stones are also available and promise an elegant tribal look, rather than a trashy one.

NEW YORK STYLE

> *"New York ladies use clothes as armor,*
> *expressive art, and weapons of seduction."*

New York Style Icons

From the classic style of Carolyn Bessette Kennedy and heiress Brooke Astor to fierce and edgy Grace Jones and Debbie Harry, many notable women have paved the way to make New York style speak for itself. The younger "It Girl" generation – path makers like Chloe Sevigny, Ashley Olsen, Zoe Kravitz, and J.Crew wondergal Jenna Lyons – push the envelope even further than their foremothers and show that if accessorized the right way, a t-shirt can scream sexy and put together. These style icons could certainly afford to clothe themselves in head-to-toe Gucci, but like most local women, they know that label whores make little fashion impact.

New York's Fashion Pedigree

Paris and London lorded over the pages of fashion magazines for almost a century, with American designers barely given a glance. But New Yorkers don't wait around for their big break. They make it happen. And in 1943, while Europe was engulfed in war, US fashion publicist Eleanor Lambert created the first ever New York Fashion Week, called *Press Week*, to lure the attention of fashion editors away from Paris, where shows were cancelled because of the Nazi occupation. The gamble paid off, and New York City became the official home to the country's top designers, from Halston, Anne Klein, Bill Blass, Oscar de la Renta, and the eccentric New Yorker Betsey Johnson in the 1960s and 1970s, followed by Donna Karan, Calvin Klein, Ralph Lauren, Marc Jacobs and Michael Kors in the 1980s and 1990s.

Downtown influences always figured heavily in New York street style, from the Punk influences of CBGB stars like Deborah Harry and Malcolm McLaren's New York Dolls to the leg warmers, parachute pants, and rah-rah skirts brought to the runway by Norma Kamali. She also invented the high-heel sneaker, an essential New York accessory if there ever was one! Manolo's came on the scene in the 1980s, but New York native Beth Levine (1914-2006) is indisputably America's First Lady of Shoe Design, creating revolutionary — yet fun — heels and boots from the 1940s through the 1970s under the label of Herbert Levine, her husband. Her creations were worn by first ladies including Jacqueline Kennedy, film stars such as Marilyn Monroe, and singers such as Barbara Streisand and Nancy Sinatra, who sang praises for boots that were "made for walking."

"I miss New York. I still love how people talk to you on the street - just assault you and tell you what they think of your jacket."

—MADONNA

Fashion by Numbers

New York City is statistically the country's largest fashion market. A majority of the fashion industry's top designers are headquartered here, including Ralph Lauren, Diane von Furstenberg, Calvin Klein, Michael Kors, Nanette Lepore, and Donna Karan. It's also where most of the top fashion magazines—like Vogue and Women's Wear Daily—capture the latest trends for their glossy pages. According to the New York City Economic Development Corp., Fashion Week generates $466M a year in city revenue, with 250 events. New York Magazine once reported that a single recent fashion show required 1,800 bobby pins and 80 bottles of hairspray.

Advice from Izzy Grinspan

In this plugged-in city, cyber-style inevitably moves to the street—or is it the other way around? As the editor of Racked NY, a website about shopping and fashion in the city, Izzy Grinspan spends her days mining the web and the city's varied neighborhoods for the latest news in local fashion, style trends, boutique openings, fashion industry drama, and of course, highlighting the twice-a-year big tent extravaganza, Fashion Week. A pop culture writer for *Salon*, *Time Out New York*, and the *Believer*, Izzy lives in ever-hip Brooklyn with her husband, cat, and a growing collection of Rachel Comey shoes.

"The clothes are made for not-perfect people. But they're pretty perfect."

—*DESIGNER ISAAC MIZRAHI ON A RE-CENT COLLECTION*

"New York women aren't afraid to look sexy and they're not afraid to look smart," notes Izzy. "This is a competitive, brash, crowded city, a city that rewards people for being bold and confident, and that translates to a fearless, expressive local style." Most real life ladies don't have an expendable income falling from thin air (like the ladies of SATC), so authentic style comes from a clever mash-up, mixing the highbrow with the lowbrow. It's best to acquire a few solid, well-made, and classic pieces that go the distance——or at least take you uptown to downtown and back again. Match that $200 cashmere cardigan with the latest H&M frock or a sexy American Apparel T, and you'll be well on your way to mastering New York style.

IZZY GRINSPAN'S WARDROBE MUST-HAVES

- Really flattering jeans – if they fit well enough, you can wear them almost anywhere
- Nice flat boots – New Yorkers walk a lot
- A trench coat – your tireless defense against bad weather
- Sunglasses
- A black cashmere sweater
- A dress that can take you from the office to drinks (it's a cliché for a reason)
- Some soft, sheer, drapey t-shirts
- A pair of trustworthy heels (again, it's a walking city!)
- A roomy leather bag
- One dress that makes you feel like a stone-cold fox
- Trademark accessory: a Smartphone, such as an iPhone or BlackBerry (New York women are constantly on the go but never sacrifice constant communication)

New York Fashion Boutiques

If you clothed the Statue of Liberty in real life, this lovely, independent New York lady would require a dress of 4,000 square yards of fabric.

They say that "clothes make the man," but when a woman gets dressed in the morning she's usually looking to alter her identity. Each day offers an opportunity for reinvention, whether it's smart and stylish worker bee or a sultry lioness. New York ladies use clothes as armor, expressive art, and weapons of seduction. With an endless supply of stylish shops for both penny pinchers and label whores, the city offers plenty of opportunities for complete transformation. Never underestimate the power of retail therapy—but don't leave home without the plastic!

OPENING CEREMONY
35 HOWARD ST
212 219 2688
CANAL ST STATION
WWW.OPENINGCEREMONY.US

This three-floor destination for cutting-edge fashion joins up-and-coming American talent with well-known international designers. You'll find Alexander Wang's tissue weight t-shirts, starting at $90, fancier labels like Toga, and funky rock star jewelry. The store's own label offers a hybrid of neo-preppy and flouncy, feminine wear. No time to head downtown? Drop by the newly-opened sister shop at the hip Ace Hotel.

OAK
28 BOND ST
212 677 1293
BLEECKER ST STATION
WWW.OAKNYC.COM

This quintessential New York store is a great place to pick up a pair of designer jeans by Acne or hand-crafted Denim & Thread. Like Opening Ceremony, Oak carries the best of local designers, but the threads skew a little younger and even more avant-garde. You'll mostly find a basic color palette of black and slate grey though the items are hardly boring.

FOLEY & CORINNA
114 STANTON ST
212 529 2338
ESSEX ST/DELANCY STATION
WWW.FOLEYANDCORINNA.COM

This shop's pretty, feminine dresses, starting at $300 are a favorite among Hollywood's A-listers for their downtown, vintage-inspired feel. This Lower East Side store is also the place to procure a perfect handbag. The beloved classic satchel comes in every imaginable color and in both small and large sizes, from $200 to $450. The large ones are perfect for New Yorkers who lug around too much stuff.

RESURRECTION VINTAGE
217 MOTT ST
212 625 1374
SPRING ST STATION
WWW.RESURRECTIONVINTAGE.COM

Fashion stylist Rachel Zoe's favorite place for designer vintage has classic pieces every nostalgic lady will love. From original Emilio Pucci silk shirts, around $450, butt-hugging riding chaps with leather details, for $800, to classic Chanel handbags and link bracelets. Owner and designer Katy Rodriguez and her partner-in-crime Mark Haddawy acquire most of their store's collectibles in Los Angeles and other CA locales.

KIRNA ZABÊTE
96 GREENE ST
212 941 9656
PRINCE ST STATION
WWW.KIRNAZABETE.COM

Owners Sasha and Beth have a simple store policy, outlined on the wall of their Soho shop: "Come in, hang out, roll up you sleeves, babies welcome, dogs welcome, beginners welcome, play dress up, try on something you can't afford, spend now, worry later, leave looking lovely." This well-curated, high-fashion mecca first opened in 1999 with the best European and American designers like Tuleh, Stella McCartney, Proenza Schouler, and Elise Overland.

TOPSHOP
478 BROADWAY
212 966 9555
CANAL ST STATION
WWW.TOPSHOP.COM

The only shop located in the U.S., this is London High Street fashion fit to walk the streets of New York, from their flirty frocks starting at $100 to their leather biker jackets for around $300. Stylish handbags and shoes, plus funky accessories guarantee that you won't leave empty-handed. On the weekends, there's always a superb DJ spinning for a party atmosphere.

STEVEN ALAN
103 FRANKLIN ST
212 343 0692
FRANKLIN ST STATION
WWW.STEVENALAN.COM

JUMELLE
148 BEDFORD AVE
718 388 9525
BROOKLYN, BEDFORD AVE STATION
WWW.SHOPJUMELLE.COM

The king of madras plaid is as popular with the uber preps as he is with the moody hipster. The New York native designer constantly sells out of staples like the classic button down shirts, from $160, and cute shirt dresses (the Loren mini dress, a perennial fave, is $225). At the Tribeca Annex you'll also find complementary labels, including Isabel Marant, A.P.C., and Engineered Garments.

Located in fashion-conscious Williamsburg, Jumelle epitomizes hip, Brooklyn style, the kind of fine clothes that look effortless enough to wear while gallivanting in the park, but sexy enough to carry you to a late-night dinner. The store is filled with a well-edited collection of 20 established American and international designers like Bodkin, Jackson, Johnston & Roe, A. Detacher, and Shabd for a wardrobe of "eclectic elegance".

BIRD

316 FIFTH AVE
718 768 4940
BROOKLYN, UNION ST STATION
WWW.SHOPBIRD.COM

This flagship shop embodies hip high-end Brooklyn style. With designers like 3.1 Phillip Lim, Acne, A.P.C., Isabel Marant, Proenza Schouler, Rachel Comey, and Thakoon, local chicks need not cross the Brooklyn Bridge for great threads. Jewelry by New York designers Etten Eller and Giles & Brother round out the collection. The LEED-certified shop is located in picturesque, eco-minded Park Slope.

DIANE VON FURSTENBERG

874 WASHINGTON ST
646 486 4800
8TH AVE/ 14TH ST STATION
WWW.DVF.COM

Many designers have tried to emulate Von Furstenberg's classic wrap dress ($300 and up), born at this flagship store and the mark of her 1970s fame. Enjoy an opulent shopping experience with a VIP dressing room and beverage service. Her trademark look hasn't gone out of style, but there's always something new among her sports, evening, and outerwear. Shoes and accessories complete the independent-lady-about-town mystique.

BERGDORF GOODMAN

754 5TH AVE
212 753 7300
5TH AVE STATION
WWW.BERGDORFGOODMAN.COM

Opened at the turn of the century, this city staple for balls-to-the-walls luxury puts other department stores to shame. You'll find haute couture fixtures like Chanel and Giorgio Armani, along with younger labels such as CREED and Michelle Obama's fave, Jason Wu. Take a full day to mine the more than 70 designer collections, represented here as well as oodles of high end contemporary wear—like Juicy Couture and 7 for all Mankind denim. If you get hungry while getting lost among the beauty, four fine restaurants offer high-class snacks and girly cocktails.

BARNEYS

660 MADISON AVE
212 826 8900
5TH AVE STATION
WWW.BARNEYS.COM

"If you're a nice person and you work hard, you get to shop at Barneys. It's the decadent reward," once said Sarah Jessica Parker. Known for their outrageous window displays and discerning fashion since 1923, this institution is guaranteed to revive even the most forlorn soul. Its cheery, endless supply of chic fashion (by the likes of Behnaz Sarafpour, Miu Miu, and Marc Jacobs) and the store's *joie to vivre* keeps shoppers spending their money, but always in good humor. Twice a year, the Chelsea location hosts its famous warehouse sale—up to 80 percent off—check their website for details.

How to Spot a Tourist

It's not just a camera slung around the neck that's a tell-tale sign. Plenty of visitors hoping to meld with the melting pot often end up sticking out more like sore thumbs. Designer label clothes and accessories are fun to own and wear but try not to go overboard. Think of your visitor wardrobe like putting together a well-balanced meal. You don't want too many of the same items on your dish! If you've got a real Prada bag (lucky you!), don't match it with the Prada shoes and the Gucci dress. Mix it up with more middle of the road items. Other visitor faux pas include incredibly light colored "mom-jeans" with sneakers, head-to-toe sports fan regalia, "crunchy" overly styled hair, scrunchies, and too much fake fur. Also avoid baring too much skin. For maximum impact pick a single part of your body to showcase—décolletage, great legs—and cover the rest up!

Luscious Lingerie

The start of any great outfit is an excellent foundation. Whether lace, silk, or satin, pretty undergarments say a lot when the lights go down and make you feel extra confident when gallivanting for a night on the town. Nothing is as tantalizing as a well-fitted bra to sculpt your décolletage with matching boy shorts or a thong that shows off your curves. Burn the granny panties and head to one of these shops for the real thing, whether it's romantic, sexy or—*wink*—mildly kinky.

"Brevity is the soul of lingerie."
—DOROTHY PARKER

AGENT PROVOCATEUR

133 MERCER ST
212 965 0229
PRINCE ST STATION
WWW.AGENTPROVOCATEUR.COM

Playful and erotic, this lingerie empire is the brain-child of Vivienne Westwood's son and his ex-wife, a top choice among celebs like Paris Hilton, Fern Britton, and Carmen Electra. Their deceptively coy "Fifi," bra, $170, a French maid-inspired pink and black number with matching panties remains a perennial bestseller. There's also more elaborate items like bone corsets, starting at $580, and the "Bomb" playsuit, reminiscent of Pink's costume from the 2010 Grammy trapeze performance. Conjure up your inner Bettie Page with sparkly pasties and high quality whips and paddles, starting at $120.

KIKI DE MONTPARNASSE

79 GREENE ST
212 965 8150
PRINCE ST STATION
WWW.KIKIDM.COM

This Soho store might do better to call itself *Kinky* de Montparnesse with its great selection of high end items for feminine and fetish fantasies. Highlights include the French Lesson panty set with mange-moi (eat me), fesse-moi (spank me), attache-moi (tie me up) silkscreened on the back for $295, lingerie of French lace and silk, bridal negligees, and elegant C-rings for your honey. Skip Tiffany's and turn your lover into a hotel room hostage with 24K gold handcuffs for $350. Or consider a handmade cat mask for $550 to get your partner purring.

Only Hearts

386 COLUMBUS AVE
212 724 5608
81ST ST/MUSEUM OF NATURAL HISTORY STATION
WWW.ONLYHEARTS.COM

Hearts are everywhere at this lovely shop that's made its name promoting the universal symbol of love for over 30 years. Classic mesh with lace trim sets in eye-popping colors start at $35 while lovely, body-hugging all silk slips are $100 (both make great bridal shower gifts). Peruse the special vintage-inspired jewelry like gold and brass heart-shaped lockets and delicate earrings; your guy may be tempted to throw one in as a token of affection.

Town Shop

2273 BROADWAY
212 787 2762
79TH ST STATION
WWW.TOWNSHOP.COM

At this 100-year-old Upper West Side shop, the city's best fitters stick to the simple motto: "Finding the perfect bra is an art, not a science." Whatever your size — from AA to JJ — the ladies here will make your beautiful body bulge in all the right places. Brands like Aubade, Cosabella, Wolford, Lejaby fill the crowded racks, and come with matching thongs or briefs. But don't be overwhelmed by the shop's huge selection; sales clerks offer plenty of one-on-one guidance.

Bra Smyth

2177 BROADWAY
212 721 5111
79TH ST STATION
WWW.BRASMYTH.COM

This store started as a mom-and-pop shop in the Bronx back in 1932. Now on the Upper West Side, it offers a more intimate place to buy brand name favorites—both practical and sexy—like Wacoal, Gossard, Chantelle, and Spanx. Whether you need to shape your silhouette for a sexy, strapless dress or create that natural-looking, attention-grabbing décolletage beneath a soft casual t-shirt, a professional fitter and tailor will have you covered.

Orchard Corset

157 ORCHARD ST
212 674 0786
ESSEX ST/DELANCY ST STATION
WWW.ORCHARDCORSET.COM

This discount family-owned shop looks like a pathological hoarder's living room with boxes of brassieres and mountains of merchandise. But they sure know boobs and how to fit a bra. The owner, a Hassidic man, will check out your rack, then steer you in the right direction. His wife lectures customers on wearing the wrong size bra, grabs a few to try, then reaches into the cups to adjust nipples. Guaranteed to perk up your girls!

LA PETITE COQUETTE

51 UNIVERSITY PL
212 473 2478
8TH ST/NYU STATION
WWW.THELITTLEFLIRT.COM

The owner of this sweet West Village shop is also
the author of *The Lingerie Handbook*, the most defini-
tive guide to under things. Carrying plenty of pretty,
romantic bra and panty sets by European designers and
beyond, this small shop is a favorite of Cindy Crawford
and the Real Housewives. Bestselling items include silky
chemises starting at $130, barely there demi cup bras by
brands like Timpa for $33, and the Bracli pearl thong,
$69, guaranteed to rub every lady the right way. A visit
here will turn any wallflower into a "little flirt."

LA PERLA

93 GREENE ST
212 219 0999
PRINCE ST STATION
WWW.LAPERLA.COM

At this Soho outpost of the popular designer chain, sales clerks will show you something pretty to wear under just about anything, like the superbly-constructed, super low cut underwire bra, $250, that makes even the most plunging neckline attainable. Lovely details adorn each one of their bras such as Chantilly lace and tulle straps. The label also pioneered the filigree-inspired jewelry lingerie collection, for those wishing to adorn her breasts in 14 carat gold thread. Who wouldn't?

ERES

621 MADISON AVE
212 223 3550
5TH AVE STATION
WWW.ERESPARIS.COM

This French label is synonymous with superior swimwear and well cut lingerie in modern fabrics like tulle, silk satin, and high quality cotton, plus chemises in silk crepe. A little bit of Paris in New York never did a girl any harm.

Sexy Shoes

No one loves shoes as much as a New York City lady. Sarah Jessica Parker fawned over her Manolos at least once in every episode of SATC, and then there's the gorgeous sight of endless designer heels in heaping piles at the Barneys annual sample sale. Fabulous, well-made shoes are an imperative in this city, since pounding the pavement is a main part of living here. New Yorkers walk everywhere, an average of four and a half miles a day, compared to the one mile average for the rest of the country. But comfy sneakers don't really make the cut in this high-styled metropolis. Sleek high boots, well-made pumps, pretty ballet flats, and sexy sandals are a must-have. Be sure you've got plenty of space in your suitcase.

CHRISTIAN LOUBOUTIN

59 HORATIO ST
212 255 1910
8TH AVE/14TH ST STATION
WWW.CHRISTIANLOUBOUTIN.COM

All ladies know how to spot a pair of Louboutins: the signature red soles. At this West Village shop, you'll find endless pairs with a fetishist appeal—most stilettos clock in at 4 ½ inches. There's sparkly platforms a drag queen would love and f**k me pumps for around $600 in red patent leather or gold sequins. Give the gamine look a go with spirited ballet flats (your arches may thank you).

JIMMY CHOO

716 MADISON AVE
212 593 0800
LEXINGTON AVE/63RD ST STATION
WWW.JIMMYCHOO.COM

It's no surprise that these serious pumps are beloved by stylish ladies everywhere. A pair of Jimmy Choos at once says "you want me" and "I'm dangerously fashionable." Whether worn day or night – strappy gladiator-style mile high sandals or a sassy peep toe pump – you'll feel unbearably confident with these girls on. A pair of Choos averages $700 a pop. Yes, they're certainly an investment – but then again, so is a boyfriend.

MANOLO BLAHNIK

31 WEST 54TH ST
212 582 3007
5TH AVE/ 53RD ST STATION
WWW.MANOLOBLAHNIK.COM

The beloved designer once said: "You put high heels on and you change." For a metamorphosis from the outside in, nothing transforms a woman into a dazzling butterfly quite like a pair of Manolos. The Spanish designer is synonymous with New York City, thanks to SATC, but real women of Gotham go nuts over these hot heels. Each pair is a little work of art fit for the MOMA and priced as such.

SIGERSON MORRISON

28 PRINCE ST
212 625 1641
PRINCE ST STATION
WWW.SIGERSONMORRISON.COM

A standard for chic, young women in New York, this British brand—founded in New York City—keeps the downtown crowd well-heeled each season. At this low-key Nolita shop you'll find a broad variety of the season's hottest styles, but it's the more "work-appropriate" pumps that have local ladies all in a tizzy. Both sophisticated and smart, a pair of these heels should make your day job a little less boring and certainly more sexy.

Jeffrey New York
449 WEST 14TH ST
212 206 1272
8TH AVE/14TH ST STATION
WWW.JEFFREYNEWYORK.COM

Though snobbery reigns at this hipper-than-thou fashion mecca, it's a haven for ladies with an insatiable shoe fetish. Housed in a pimped-out converted warehouse, the space caters to the proverbial Cosmo-sipping fashionista with a well-curated selection of Prada, D&G, Manolo and Gucci. Any lady with a high credit limit should certainly have a grand time here.

Iris
827 WASHINGTON ST
212 645 0950
8TH AVE/14TH ST STATION
WWW.IRISNYC.NET

This cool shop carries the entire line, each and every season, of labels like Marc Jacobs, Veronique Branquinho, Paul Smith, Viktor & Rolf and Chloé Chausseures. With a factory in Venice, Italy that produces many of the labels stocked at the store, this is a haven for women looking for that difficult to find pair —or just something completely different.

Kate Spade
454 BROOME ST
212 274 1991
SPRING ST STATION
WWW.KATESPADE.COM

Classic ballet flats with adornments, cute peep toes, and candy-colored pumps—all starting at around $300—sit on bright green astro turf shelves at this cheerful Soho shop. Spade, a New Yorker, is famous for her perky, feel good, functional accessories. The designer first made a splash with her handbags, which are still a worthy investment. The classic boxy Quinn bag has a makeover each season in colors like canary yellow and the roomy Stevie looks pretty in red patent leather (both start at $300).

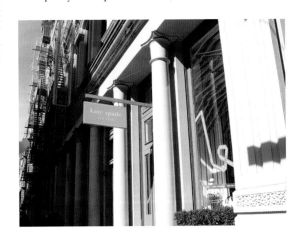

BARNEY'S SHOE DEPARTMENT

660 MADISON AVE
212 826 8900
5TH AVE STATION
WWW.BARNEYS.COM

Barneys is famous for its edit of the best shoe stores from Madison Avenue to the Meatpacking District, which has caused women many a shoe-gasm. The A-list designers include Balenciaga, Fendi, Givenchy, PRADA, Louffer Randal, See by Chloe, etc. There's nary a practical pair here. Instead you'll find footwear fit for a night owl – feathered, spangled, sparkly, with metaphorical bells and whistles

10022—SHOES (Saks Fifth Avenue Shoe Department)

611 5TH AVE
212 753 4000
47TH – 50TH ST/ROCKEFELLER CENTER STATION
WWW.SAKSFIFTHAVENUE.COM

"I still have my feet on the ground,
I just wear better shoes."
—OPRAH WINFREY

Get on the exclusive elevator located on the main floor for an express ride directly to the 8th level, the heart and sole of this elegant landmark store (the U.S. postal service even provided this shoe destination with its very own zip code). Give yourself several hours to browse the latest in luscious footwear by the likes of Chloe, Miu Miu, and PRADA.

Personal Shopping Consultants

New York is an exquisite place to shop, with thousands of retail stores at every price point and style. Though it's a dream for the shopaholic it can be a bit daunting for people who get overwhelmed by infinite choices. If you're one of the latter, consider the help of a personal shopper to develop your sense of style and keep you on track so you don't lose out on even one not-to-be-missed store.

PLANET STYLE CONCIERGE
WWW.PLANETSTYLECONCIERGE.COM

Feeling a little accessory-impaired? This agency will help you master the fine art of belts, bags, shoes, jewelry, and scarves in their Accessory 101 tutorial. The agency is also happy to take visitors on a gallivant along Fifth Avenue and Madison, or any other section of the city that's fashionably favored.

CHIC INSPIRATION
WWW.CHICINSPIRATION.COM

Ella Goldin, who began working as a fashion consultant in New York over ten years ago has a cure for your ailing closet and promises to make getting dressed in the morning stress free. Her agency also organizes tours through the New York Shopping Tour company which hits beloved boutique neighborhoods like Nolita, Soho, and the East Village.

UNIQUE & CHIC
WWW.UNIQUE-CHIC.COM

Purchasing gifts can be a challenge—Madrid native Rosalia Arteche is here to the rescue. If you run out of time to find a little token of affection for your lover, consider her services. Arteche's shopping tours are also unique since they include sightseeing of lesser known city spots and a meal at a fabulous restaurant. Available in English, Spanish, and French.

MARGARET SHRUM, THE LINGERIE GODDESS
WWW.THELINGERIEDIET.COM

Why oh why do some of the most fashionable ladies wear such hideously, unsexy lingerie? That's what the lovely Shrum thought when she started her lingerie consulting company. Her Essential Foundation Makeover provides four hours of assistance. After a lingerie questionnaire and an assessment of your current collection, she'll take you to her favorite shops—like Agent Provacateur and La Perla—and help you bring sexy back to your under things. Gentlemen, she can also help you pick out a little something tasteful or naughty for your special lady.

Shopping Guides

New Yorkers are good at getting a lot for very little! Most material girls take great pride in their ability to troll local blogs and listings so they can snag a few pairs at Jeffrey's annual 50% off designer shoe sale, or purchase Theory frocks in bulk. For weekly shopping information—like sample sales and new store openings—*Time Out New York* magazine is always a great bet. For the newsstand price of $3.99, you'll get some of the most up-to-date listings. Blogs are an excellent source as well. *Racked NY, Daily Candy,* and *New York* magazine also have frequent updates for anyone seeking out a hefty dose of retail therapy. If you must get a guide book for your shopping adventures *eat.shop nyc: A Curated Guide of Inspired and Unique Locally Owned Eating and Shopping Establishments in Manhattan, Brooklyn, Queens, the Bronx, and Staten Island* and *Where Magazine's New York City Shop!: Great Shopping Wherever* are useful. As is the *Not For Tourist* (NFT) series. You can pick up many of these guides at the Strand Bookstore, a New York institution, and a shopping experience in itself.

"Style is simple. You wear it. It doesn't wear you,"
— NEW YORK DESIGNER JACKIE ROGERS, WHOSE CLIENTS INCLUDED KENNEDY ONASSIS.

Sartorial Inspiration

True style is hard to define, and even harder to package and sell. That's why Scott Schuman's blog "The Sartorialist" is so fabulous. There is nothing but beautiful photos of people he passes on the streets of New York (also Paris, Milan, London…) whose style he admires, whether casual, sporty, or dressy. He has nothing to sell, doesn't ask his subjects about the labels they're wearing, and aside from a few comments on what drew him to a particular look, keeps the chatter to a minimum. www.thesartorialist.blogspot.com

PART IV

Get in the Mood

Anticipation...totally underrated yet surprisingly effective for getting yourself in that perfectly naughty Manhattan state of mind. Indulge in the hedonistic side of local culture, shop for something that makes you blush, and pique your libido by learning some sexy moves. And whether you dare to delve any further into this guide or not, we guarantee that after this chapter it won't be because you're not in the mood.

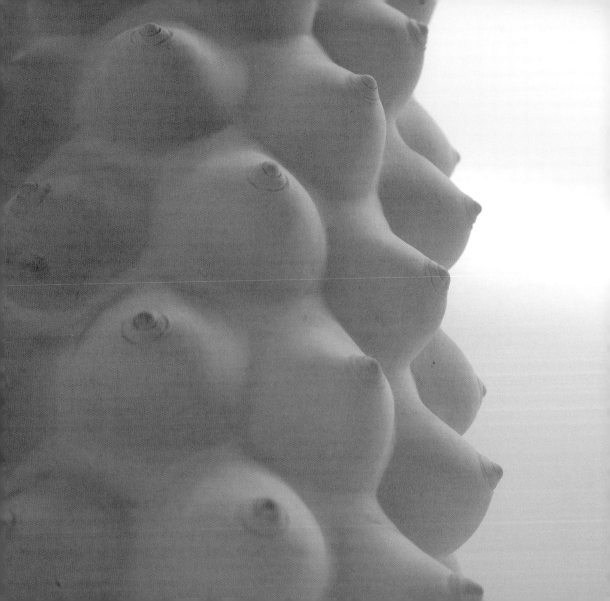

NAUGHTY CULTURE

> *"Some of the most famous masterpieces*
> *ever created pay homage to the human body."*

As America's "Capital of Culture", there's no better place than New York City to immerse yourself in the rich multicultural stew of art, music, theatre, dance, cinema and cuisine. With such an astounding bounty of treasures at your feet, you can count on finding your naughty delight. After all, nothing is sexier than a woman ignited with a passion for new discoveries.

Naughty Masterpieces

With a taste for the bold and an inclination towards the subversive, the New York art scene has always been willing to push the boundaries and challenge the status quo. So it should come to no surprise that titillating sculptures and suggestive paintings have made their way into the venerable halls of the city's finest art museums. No need to avert your eyes…the other museum patrons can't tell if you're flushed with desire or blushing with modesty.

MUSEUM OF MODERN ART

11 W 53RD ST
212 708 9400
47/50TH ST ROCKEFELLER CENTER STATION
WWW.MOMA.ORG

An afternoon at the MoMA can inspire the most unusual sexual musings. If you find a fellow tourist or a too-young-for-you-to-seriously-consider (if you weren't on vacation) art student contemplating a work of art, all the more reason to strike up a conversation. There is certainly no shortage of carnal pleasures to contemplate, including the plastic sex appeal of Roy Lichtenstein's *Girl with Ball*, Gustav Klimt's *Hope II* featuring a rare artistic depiction of pregnancy, or James Rosenquist's *Marilyn Monroe I*, a graphic commentary on the ubiquitous sex symbol featured in more than 15 of the museum's works of art.

Naughty Tip:
Late Nights at the MoMA

MoMA stays open until 8:45pm every Thursday, Friday and Saturday in July and August, and admission is free every Friday night from 4-8pm. Enjoy a sunset stroll through the galleries, followed by a glass of wine in the museum's Bar Room, open until 10:30pm. What better way to pick up a fellow art-lover?

HAYDEN PLANETARIUM
175 CENTRAL PARK WEST
212 769 5000
81ST ST STATION
WWW.HAYDENPLANETARIUM.ORG

A trip to the planetarium always puts us in the mood to make out like teenagers on a school trip. When the lights go down, engage in some discreet fondling with your date or hold hands under the stars with a perfect stranger. The Journey to the Stars space show will transport you from New York City to a galaxy far, far away while the SonicVision show is a trippy experience for music lovers.

METROPOLITAN MUSEUM OF ART
1000 FIFTH AVE, 86TH ST STATION
212 535 7710
WWW.METMUSEUM.ORG

Looking for a new angle on art appreciation? Some of the most famous masterpieces ever created pay homage to the human body, and you'll find the best of them at the Met. Parmigianino, Matisse, Rodin and Renoir offer their own take on both the male and female forms, and how passionately they go together. No need to tell anyone you're here for the sculpted bottoms and erotically-charged photos…it can be your little secret.

Al Fresco Inspiration

THE CLOISTERS
99 MARGARET CORBIN DRIVE
212 923 3700
190TH ST STATION
WWW.METMUSEUM.ORG/CLOISTERS

Overlooking the Hudson River in Manhattan's Fort Tryon Park, these enclosed medieval-style gardens featuring elements from real French cloisters form a peaceful refuge. But you don't have to make like a monk to enjoy this off-the-beaten-path setting favored by privacy-seeking lovers.

BROOKLYN BOTANIC GARDEN
1000 WASHINGTON AVE
718 623 7200
BROOKLYN, EASTERN PARKWAY/BROOKLYN MUSEUM STATION
WWW.BBG.ORG

Stroll through the Cranford Rose Garden in spring or make your way through the perfectly manicured Japanese Hill-and-Pond Garden. If you're not already in love, you will be when you get here. This 52-acre "living museum" is without a doubt the most romantic getaway in all five boroughs.

CENTRAL PARK
FROM 59TH ST TO 110TH ST, AND 5TH AVENUE TO CENTRAL PARK WEST.
212 310 6600
WWW.CENTRALPARKNYC.ORG

Savvy New Yorkers escape the boom boxes, skaters and dogs in the "quiet zones" of Manhattan's famous 843-acre park. Strawberry Fields (west side between 71st and 74th Streets) was the preferred oasis of one of the most sensual and creative couples ever – John Lennon and Yoko Ono. Or try reciting erotic poetry to your lover in the Shakespeare Garden (on the west side between 79th and 80th Streets), an informal garden with rustic benches and roses intertwined in the fence.

STATEN ISLAND FERRY
4 SOUTH ST
WHITEHALL ST STATION
WWW.SIFERRY.COM

While the rest of the passengers are busy admiring the sweeping views of lower Manhattan's skyline and Lady Liberty, you and the ladies have 25 leisurely minutes to check out the talent aboard the free Staten Island Ferry cruise. If you're already in play, position yourself and your man starboard (right) side for the best views. It's one of the most romantic cruises you'll ever take without spending a dime.

Extra Naughty Culture

MUSEUM OF SEX

233 FIFTH AVENUE
212 689 6337
28TH ST STATION
WWW.MUSEUMOFSEX.COM

Located in an area formerly called the Tenderloin, known for its bordellos and seedy saloons, the Museum of Sex resides in what looks like a sleek office building on Fifth Avenue. Still, the presence of the museum does tend to raise a few eyebrows in this otherwise business-oriented area. Since it opened its doors in 2002, MoSex has expanded its collection to include over 15,000 artifacts including works of art, photographs, costumes and clothing, and technological inventions. With the minimalist white rooms, fluorescent lighting and sterile glass cases showcasing everything from vintage vibrators to close-up photos of STD viruses, the museum is more Sex Ed than sexy. But even ladies who think they've seen it all can marvel at homemade sex machines, caress the male and female RealDolls, and wax nostalgic over the classic American porn magazines.

Broads on Broadway

On Broadway the world really is a stage, whether you are walking along the famous street or already seated inside one of its 40-plus theatrical venues. In a place where city zoning dictates that all storefronts around Times Square must be done in lights and neon, personal zoning dictates that anything goes. Here is the place to shine forth your unique light and unfetter your inner diva. Broadway's Theatre District fans out from The Great White Way (42nd to 53rd Streets) like a flamenco dancer's skirt. How you approach Broadway can be as diverse as the international cast of characters who have graced New York theatre since its evolution in the early 19th century.

Doing Broadway like a New York Lady

New York women are self-assured and comfortable with their own company, and with such a large selection of shows, if you go solo you can pick a performance that closely fits your own individual mood (perhaps it's *Jersey Boys*, *Wicked*, *Phantom of the Opera*, or *God of Carnage?*). If you go on a date, a romantic or comedic piece might be just the ticket, and offers sexy and smart after show conversation (*Venus in Fur* anyone?). And, if you go with girlfriends, Broadway is rich with intelligent and sassy performances by and about strong women (consider *Girls Night, Love, Loss and What I Wore,* or *Naked Boys Singing!*).

Picking a Show & Getting Tickets like a Local

Serious Broadway aficionados save their heels for the show and go to Broadway.com or www. TicketMaster.com/Broadway/showlistings for ticket discounts and deals. Broadway.com is the most comprehensive site and also offers show-hotel packages. Though not necessarily bargains, the packages offer pairings that do Broadway in style. If Broadway is your *raison d'etre* for coming to New York, this may be the way to go, be it solo or for a romantic *tête-à-tête*.

And if you really want to show off your heels and be spontaneous on Times Square, head to TKTS, under the big red stairs, at 47th & Broadway for same-day, discounted tickets (www.tdf.org). Shows usually run eight times a week during six days, with matinees on Wednesdays, Saturdays, and Sundays. Most theatres close on Mondays…the cast members need their beauty rest, after all.

Theatrical Dress Codes

Broadway is the place to let out your inner muse, to dress as you want, however flamboyant or discrete. The world is a stage and the audience is given as much expression as the actors. Theatergoers dress down in jeans and polar fleece or dress up in silk dresses, hand-embroidered shawls, and Manolo Blahnik heels. Express yourself and give your own unique regards to Broadway.

Classic New York Cinema

THE ZIEGFELD THEATRE
141 WEST 54TH STREET
212 307 1862
7TH AVENUE/5TH AVENUE STATIONS
WWW.CINEMATREASURES.ORG/THEATER/12

The original 1928 Ziegfeld Theatre was at 6th Avenue and 54th Street. It was controversially torn down in 1966 and in 1969 the current palace cinema opened in its honor a few hundred feet away. Named after savvy entertainment businessman, Florenz Ziegfeld, the theatre reminds us of his legacy as the "glorifier of the American girl." Still whispering the presence of elegant divas past, from Fanny Brice to Audrey Hepburn, this is the place to don your rhinestones and vintage attire and be a part of the elegance of one of the last of the grand movie palaces of crimson carpets, red velvet seats, ballroom chandeliers, roaring Twenties-styled ticket booths, and heavy curtains that open and close each screening.

> "Roaming the streets of New York, we encountered many examples of this delightful quality of New Yorkers, forever on their toes, violently, restlessly involving themselves in the slightest situation brought to their attention, always posing alternatives, always ready with an answer or an argument."
>
> —JESSICA MITFORD, FROM HONS AND REBELS

Naughty Literary Events

THE HAPPY ENDING LOUNGE

302 BROOME ST
212 334 9676
BOWERY OR 2ND AVENUE STATIONS
WWW.HAPPYENDINGLOUNGE.COM

This former massage parlor on the Lower East Side is now home to a fun and sexy club with a diverse clientele. The intimate, red-velvet décor and retro kitsch style of the lower lounge, throwbacks to the titillatingly seedy atmosphere of Sinatra's pre-Giuliani New York, are the perfect setting for the free naughty events hosted here, including:

- **The Red Umbrella Diaries** "Stories of Sex & Money", hosted by sex worker activist Audacia Ray, gives the audience an insider look at the lives of sex workers of both genders, and challenges you to question your own assumptions about sex work. Note that 15% of the bar tab is donated to sex positive charitable organizations (first Thursday of the month at 8pm, www.redumbrellaproject.com).

- **Pleasure Salon** "A place for the open exchange of ideas and sensual expression" bringing together members of diverse sex-positive communities including BDSM, swinger, LGBT, sex-activist, nudist, sex-magic, polyamory, Pagan, radical faerie, tantra, dark odyssey, sex-blogger and others whose passion is sex (first Wednesday of the month from 6pm, www.pleasuresalon.com).

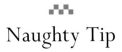

Naughty Tip

Get there early, seating is limited.

Cultural Tours

If you're reading this book, you're probably a savvy traveler who can find her way around a big city. But New York isn't just a big city – it's *the* big city. So if you decide you want to take a break and let someone else do the legwork, there's no shame in kicking up your feet and going along for the ride.

SEX AND THE CITY HOTSPOTS

NEAR 5TH AVE & 58TH ST
212 209 3370
WWW.SCREENTOURS.COM

Though it may seem cheesy to some, the *Sex and the City* tour is one of the most popular attractions for visitors to the Big Apple who want to hit the spots that Carrie and the ladies frequented on the famed TV show. You'll down Cosmos, munch on cupcakes from the Magnolia Bakery and stop into the Pleasure Chest where Charlotte picked up her Rabbit. Savvy fans can find all the spots on this tour themselves, but if you don't want to deal with the hassle of planning, don a boa and just go with the flow. Tours daily at 11am and 3pm, tickets $44.

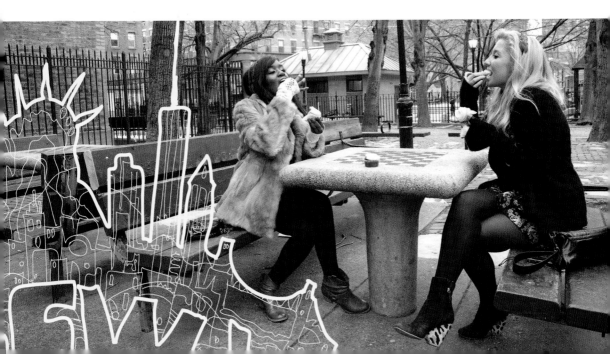

CLASSIC NEW YORK MOVIE SITES TOURS

NEAR BROADWAY AND 51ST STREET
212 209 3370
WWW.SCREENTOURS.COM

The same company brought back our favorite tour featuring iconic New York movie locations from *Breakfast at Tiffany's*, *Taxi Driver*, *Superman*, Woody Allen's *Manhattan*, *Wall Street*, *Stella*, *Moonstruck* and *West Side Story*. Movie screens onboard the bus show the movie scenes as you pass each location. Tours every first and third Sunday at noon, tickets $40.

ROMANCE OVER MANHATTAN HELICOPTER TOUR

800 213 2474
WWW.TRUSTEDTOURS.COM

Board a private helicopter and see NYC from a new vantage point as your pilot whisks you past the Statue of Liberty and over Central Park. Zoom in for a bird's eye view of the bankers on Wall Street and experience the city as you've never seen it before. Although it's pricey ($995) this is one flight you'll never forget.

FAMOUS FAT DAVE'S FOOD TOUR

646 496 6540
WWW.FAMOUSFATDAVE.COM

Your driver may be a little bloated, but that's because he's well-versed in all the culinary delights this city has to offer. Dave will pick you up in an old-fashioned checker cab and take you to some of the most amazing, underground eateries you've never heard about. Gastronomic delights are around every corner as you feast on the same foods that Anthony Bourdain enjoyed. Don't get too full -- you might want to get a little frisky in the back of the taxi!

THE HALF MOON CRUISE

E 23RD ST & FDR DRIVE
212 691 6693
WWW.NEWYORKBOOZECRUISE.COM
WWW.ROCKSOFF.COM

Although the name Booze Cruise may be a tad off-putting for cultured ladies, rest assured that nothing takes away from the views of Manhattan's glittering skyline as you cruise along the harbor. You can charter a private yacht if you want to keep it in the family, or join one of the lunch, dinner, or rock concert cruises to mingle and party with new friends. Prices start at $49, including buffet and two drinks.

The Art of Hailing a Cab

A Few Basics

The yellow light on the top of every yellow New York Cab is in fact not one but three lights. There is a center light, with the taxi's medallion number, flanked on either side by two yellow lights. When only the middle light is illuminated, the cab is available. Otherwise, when there is no light, or only the 2 side lights or all lights are illuminated, the cab is not free. Also, note that all New York Cabs take credit cards.

The Steps

1. Take note of your surroundings, watch out for traffic and position yourself in front of other cab seekers (unless they are elderly or infirm).

2. Identify an available cab and raise your hand as if it were an old friend who is seeking you out (no need to whistle or start signaling for air traffic). The secret here is confidence; remember that you have a right to a cab as much as any other person. In fact, New York City Fashion Protocol demands that cabs be given in first priority to women in designer shoes, even ahead of women in labor and other medical emergencies.

3. Once in the cab, tell the driver the address and if you know it specify the two cross streets (For example, "I'm going to Saks, 5th Avenue between 49th and 50th").

Naughty Lingo

The language of love is usually easy to interpret, but New Yorkers do have their own ways of saying things that you should be familiar with. Do you want to share a cab? At the end of a night partying in NYC a potential suitor may ask you if you want to take a taxi together. Never mind that you're heading uptown and he lives in Brooklyn – this is code for "let's go home together," or at least do a little kissing in the back seat. If you're not into it, simply hail your own cab.

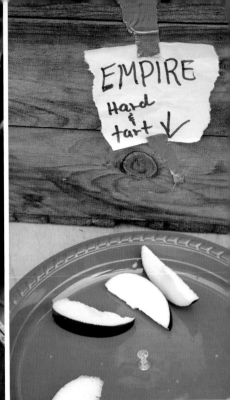

EMPIRE
Hard
&
tart ✓

NEW YORK NIBBLES

Fashions in sin change." —LILLIAN HELLMAN

If you have to ask what's naughty about food, then take a seat: you have much to learn. Forget trying to impress the locals with your knowledge of foreign films, indie music, or the latest underground fashion designers. Food is the new sexy. Just look at the popularity of sexy chef shows and proliferation of gourmet food shops if you have any doubts. The cosmopolitan city has always been an international feast of tempting foods and colorful culinary specialties from around the world, but New Yorkers hip to the Slow Food, Buy Local, and Buy Fresh movements can be scoped out in the city's many farmers markets and specialty gourmet shops. Rub shoulders with serious foodies and celebrated chefs while gathering ingredients for a luscious picnic…or phone numbers for your next date.

Union Square Farmers Market

UNION SQUARE WEST
14TH STREET UNION SQUARE STATION
WWW.CENYC.ORG/GREENMARKET

If Eve wanted the ultimate apples, Union Square would be her garden. Farmers and New Yorkers crowd in to exchange the freshest Hudson Valley seasonal produce, like spring greens, pit fruits, tomatoes, squashes, and colorful root vegetables. There are also wild berry spreads, honey in its honeycombs, and spicy hot cider. Open Monday, Wednesday, Friday and Saturday.

Chelsea Market

75 9TH AVENUE, BETWEEN 15TH AND 16TH STREETS
212 243 6005
14TH STREET STATION
WWW.CHELSEAMARKET.COM

The upscale Chelsea Market offers the full sensual indulgence of New York's premium edible luxuries. The former19th-century cookie factory houses Jacques Torres Chocolate, Eleni's perky one-of-a-kind cupcakes, Hale and Hearty Soups, Lucy's Whey cheeses, the Nutbox, and the Manhattan Fruit Exchange. Take your market catch to the café tables along the central passageways, where the walls are lined with romantic photographs of stolen kisses and flirtatious glances.

Essex Street Market

120 ESSEX STREET
DELANCY STREET STATION
WWW.ESSEXSTREETMARKET.COM

Open every day but Sunday, this classic European-styled covered market founded in the 1940s originally reflected the international foods of the Lower East Side's Italian and Jewish residents. Today strong Latino flavors dominate along with local foods. At Shopsin's you can try and charm the famously feisty chef into cooking up one of his delicious original dishes.

Grand Central Market

87 E. 42ND STREET, ENTER ON LEXINGTON AVENUE SIDE
GRAND CENTRAL 42ND STREET STATION
WWW.GRANDCENTRALTERMINAL.COM

This elegant Art Deco train station hosts a colorful market where merchants with a warm, no-nonsense New York cheer will help you select artisanal picnic ingredients from Wild Edible's produce, Murray's Real Salami, and Zaro's Bread Basket. Pick up a few aphrodisiacal oysters downstairs at the Oyster Bar & Restaurant, or for truly creamy, worth-the-calories desserts, savor a pastry from Corrado Bread & Pastry.

S.O.S. Chefs

104 AVENUE B
212.505.5813
1ST AVENUE STATION
WWW.SOS-CHEFS.COM

Kalustyan's

123 LEXINGTON AVENUE
212 685 3451
28TH STREET STATION
WWW.KALUSTYANS.COM

"Almost anything you can dream of we can find," is the driving motive behind S.O.S. Chefs of New York. Founded by Tunisian-born, Atef Boulaabi, S.O.S. Chefs is famous for locating exotic, tantalizing, gourmet food ingredients from the most authentic sources around the globe, such as saffron, truffles, foie gras, premium vanilla beans, and argan oil, a North African specialty known both for culinary nuttiness and for enhancing beauty. Look for the sign engraved in the pavement signaling that strong desires are handled with discretion.

Called "one of New York's most fragrant and exotic markets" by the New York Times, Kalustyan's has been enticing locals for over 70 years. That first swing of the door opens to at least 30 distinct and intoxicating smells, from truffles to olives to exotic herbs, teas, and spices. Mingle amongst the rice grains to discover at least twenty varieties (saffron rice, forbidden rice, green bamboo rice), multiple jellies, smoked sea salts, chutneys, rubs, and pastes (including kebab pastes).

Russ & Daughters

179 EAST HOUSTON STREET
212 475 4880
2ND AVENUE STATION
WWW.RUSSANDDAUGHTERS.COM

Russ & Daughters have been "appetizing New York since 1914." Known aphrodisiacs abound here, such as caviars of several varieties, salaciously salted fishes, and even handmade chocolates in a delightful juxtaposition for such a small space. One lovesick gent even had the engagement ring for his sweetie slipped into the wraps of the famous Super Heeb sandwich— a bagel with white fish salad, horseradish cream cheese and wasabi flying-fish roe—to pop the question.

Flower Power Herbs & Roots, Inc.

406 EAST 9TH STREET, BETWEEN AVENUE A AND 1ST AVENUE
212 982 6444
ASTOR PLACE/8TH STREET STATION
WWW.FLOWERPOWER.NET

Here, the Earth Goddess rules in a cozy, wall-to-wall plant magic setting open everyday from 12-7 pm. You'll find the highest quality, organic flowers, herbs, roots, leaves, and seeds in their most natural state. Some salves to consider: Breast Cream, Buzz Off, Calm Balm, and Flim Flam Jam. The Wise Women and Green Witches at hand can knowledgeably direct you toward the right love spell, confidence booster, or solo sailing salve.

"When it's three o' clock in New York, it's still 1938 in London."
—BETTE MIDLER

Street Eats

New Yorkers are in a hurry. Places to go, people to see. So it's no surprise that the city is full of places to catch a quick bite, from the ubiquitous food carts on almost every corner to the neighborhood delis and pizza stands. Here are a few of our favorite addresses.

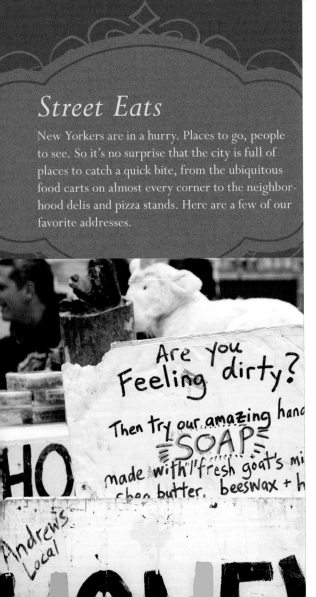

HOTDOGS

SHAKE SHACK
MADISON SQUARE PARK, AT EAST 23RD STREET AND MADISON AVENUE
212 889 6600
WWW.SHAKESHACK.COM

If all those hot dog carts are making you hungry, head to this modern day "roadside" burger stand in Madison Square Park to get your fix. You'll get to bond with the locals and other visitors lined up outside in all seasons, waiting patiently for their Shack-cago Dog, served on a poppy-seed bun and topped with relish, onion, tomato, cucumber and pickle. Just make sure to hold the onions if that handsome gentleman offers to let you go in front of him.

FALAFEL

AZURI CAFÉ
465 WEST 51ST STREET
212 262 2920
50TH STREET STATION
WWW.AZURICAFE.COM

A favorite local's hangout as much for the fresh and tasty ingredients as for the witty service and clientele, Azuri Café also produces some of the tastiest falafel this side of the Atlantic. Owner Ezra Cohen runs a kosher and cash only small space with big flavor and heart. As their takeout menu states, "…to eat Azuri food is like reaching the promise land."

PIZZA-BY-THE-SLICE

CAFÉ DANIELLO'S
1072 2ND AVENUE
212 752 5710
LEXINGTON AVENUE STATION
WWW.CAFEDANIELLOS.ORDERSVC.COM

New Yorkers are still debating who has the best pizza in Manhattan, with historic Lombardi's on Spring Street at the top of most lists for authentic Neapolitan pies. But for ladies just looking for a quickie slice of cheesy heaven, Daniello's has the best-dressed and tastiest pizzas served by the slice, with five different varieties top-loaded on a thin chewy crust.

BAGELS

MURRAY'S BAGELS
500 AVENUE OF THE AMERICAS
212 462 2830
WEST 14TH STREET STATION
WWW.MURRAYSBAGELS.COM

Follow the strong scent of doughy goodness – or the line of artsy, fashion-conscious locals – to this traditional bagel shop in Greenwich Village, where you'll find over a dozen varieties, each one blessed with a shiny, crunchy crust and chewy, full-flavored interior. Open for breakfast and lunch.

Gourmet Food Trucks

While food carts have kept time-strapped New Yorkers on-the-go fed for decades with hot dogs and gyros, demanding foodies can now rejoice in the recent proliferation of mobile gourmet food trucks serving an impressive range of delectable goodies at a fraction of what you'd pay in a restaurant. Twitter has become the best place to find the latest trucks on the scene, and where to find them. Favorites include the Rickshaw Dumpling Truck (@RickshawTruck), Papa Perrone's (@PapaPerrone), Go Burger (@GoBurger), Street Sweets (@streetsweets), the Bistro Truck (@bistrotruck) and the Big Gay Ice Cream Truck (@biggayicecream).

NAUGHTY SHOPPING

"Every city girl has her
"special drawer" by her bedside."

Art & Literature

Sophisticated NYC women know where to go when they need a fix of erotic art or reading material. Now you'll know all the right places, too, when you check out the following suggestions. Hunting down some of these places can be half the fun, leave your inhibitions back at the hotel room and happy exploring!

BLUESTOCKINGS

172 ALLEN STREET
212 777 6028
2ND AVE STATION
WWW.BLUESTOCKINGS.COM

More than a bookstore, this space is also a café and activist center where you'll find 6000 titles including tomes on gender studies, sexual liberation, feminism and even some "smutty fiction." Stop by the organic café and stay for events, readings and workshops. Surprisingly, this radical bookstore is actually quite cozy. If you're looking for the latest Oprah pick, go elsewhere, but if you're looking to stumble upon a cool zine, this is the place for you. Go to explore and leave just a little bit more enlightened!

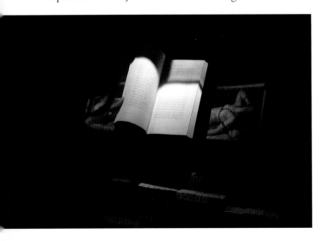

BABELAND

43 MERCER ST
212 966 2120
CANAL ST STATION
WWW.BABELAND.COM

With its clean, colorful displays, knowledgeable staff and girl-powered atmosphere, this sex shop could make even the most hesitant ladies feel right at home. Babeland hosts frequent workshops and events, and are always happy to offer how-to advice for everything from the candy-colored vibrators to the more risqué toys (restraints, butt plugs or strap-ons). Other locations at 94 Rivington Street and 462 Bergen Street in Brooklyn.

EROTICS GALLERY

41 UNION SQ W
212 633 2241
UNION SQARE STATION
WWW.EROTICRARITIES.COM

This small space features everything from pinup girl posters to Japanese Shunga erotic art woodblock prints and paintings. Started in 1975, the gallery provides a forum for budding contemporary artists as well as for erotica of a historical nature. Curator Edie Solow has amassed an international collection that is on view and includes fornicating frogs and erotic jewelry. And unlike in a museum, everything here is for sale. The gallery is by appointment only from Monday to Friday most afternoons, so be sure to call ahead.

Vixens
Neighbor
Visitors
YOU ARE SEXY—
THE WHOLE OF YOU
INSIDE AND OUT.
OUR NEW BOOK
[MOREGASM]
WAS WRITTEN FOR YOU!
www.babeland.com
Sensualists
Divas
Neophy
Come

Toys for Her

When it comes to their sex toys, NYC women aren't shy. Every city girl has her "special drawer" by her bedside, and knows the right places to go to keep it stocked with the most erotic and intriguing devices. Even if you're a first-time buyer, all of these stores will make you feel right at home.

Sex Toy Shopping for the Shy

If you've ever stood in front of a sex toy shop and been too embarrassed to go in or if you've resigned yourself to ordering items of an adult nature over the Internet, then the services of Ducky Doolittle, sex educator, speaker and author, could do you a world of good. Ducky provides one-on-one and group tours of adult shops. She'll show you which products will suit you best and helps you get over the fear that everyone is staring. And if you like, she'll even provide tips on how to introduce the toys you buy into your bedroom routine. www.duckydoolittle.com

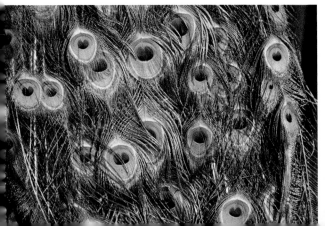

COME AGAIN

353 E 53RD ST
212 308 9394
LEXINGTON/3RD AVENUE 51ST ST STATION

Enter this Sutton Place shop and you might be taken aback by the wide array of bachelorette party novelty items. But don't worry – go past the plastic penises to find the best selection of "how-to" books and female-centric erotica in New York City. Come again has kept customers coming since its inception in 1981 with its friendly staff ready to make everyone feel at ease, even if you've never set foot in a sex shop before. In addition to the multi-media entertainment and adult party supplies, you'll find a room of sexy lingerie, S&M gear, naughty costumes, retro pulp books, stainless steel dongs and the famous Rabbit vibrator. Gentlemen will find kitsch G-string undies featuring animal faces with extra long noses.

EVE'S GARDEN

119 W 57TH ST, 12TH FLOOR
800 848 3837
57TH ST STATION
WWW.EVESGARDEN.COM

If you desire discretion when shopping for adult toys, then Eve's Garden is the place for you. Hidden inside a midtown, high-rise office building, customers avoid the hustle and bustle of a storefront location and are free to browse and ask questions in an elegant environment. If the store feels a little short on flair, it makes up for it with a solid selection of toys, books, DVDs and lotions. Dell Williams, the self-described "Gardenkeeper" of the store, has been in business since 1974. While this isn't the place to pick up penis novelty items, if you're in the market for your first vibrator or some friendly advice on all things sensual, then make your way to this high-class establishment.

Coco de Mer

236 ELIZABETH ST
212 966 9069
2ND AVE STATION
WWW.COCODEMERUSA.COM

Naughty, cheeky, luxurious and decadent, this store has everything a sexy lady needs to survive in the city. From high-end lingerie by Stella McCartney to wax massage candles, you'll indulge your senses as you shop for the perfect item. The store features works by local NYC artists as well as its own line of designer sex toys, some featuring materials like jade and onyx. Come in and have your curiosity piqued!

The Pleasure Chest

156 7TH AVE SOUTH
212 242 2158
WEST 4TH ST STATION
WWW.THEPLEASURECHEST.COM

Everyone from NYU students and Sex and the City fans to mature couples and those with a penchant for the deviant side will eventually end up at this brightly-lit and fun neighborhood favorite. The store offers everything from novelty note cards to toys like the infamous Rabbit. The good selection guarantees any girl can find a gift for herself that will keep on giving.

Ricky's

590 BROADWAY
212 226 5552
BROADWAY LAFAYETTE STATION
WWW.RICKYSNYC.COM

For those ladies looking for sex toys without the whole adult store experience, Ricky's is a no-brainer. This vibrant and always crowded chain store stocks everything from high-end hair care supplies to makeup, but the back area behind the curtain is where you'll find a decent selection of lubes, lotions and vibes. In October, the store transforms into a Halloween mecca – this is the place to pick up a naughty nurse uniform or a skimpy French maid costume. Other Manhattan locations listed on the website.

Shag

108 ROEBLING STREET
347 721 3302
BROOKLYN, BEDFORD STATION
WWW.WELOVESHAG.COM

Shag might look like just another shop selling clothes and quirky items, but the subtle tone of sexuality becomes more overt as one's eye wanders over the bath products, jewelry, sheets, and dresses to find a selection of discreetly packaged sex toys and other intimacy items. Shag's own line of products includes handcrafted platinum silicone and ceramic dildos and plugs, but the shop also sells products from select local artists whose work deals with sexuality.

Naughty Extra

More than just a store, Shag also hosts art expositions, offers custom casting of intimate body parts, and conducts workshops such as Penis Wrangling, Pole Dancing, Intro to Rope Bondage, Shaggin' Mama Moves, and Couples Massage.

PINK PUSSY CAT BOUTIQUE

355 5TH AVE
718 369 0088
BROOKLYN, 4TH AVE/NINTH ST STATION
WWW.PINKPUSSYCAT.COM

Ladies who want to feed their inner naughty kitty should make the trip to this jewel-box sized sex toy store. Tucked in a row of shops in fashionable Park Slope, the store caused some controversy when it first opened, as it's located across from a school (scandalous!). Still, the local mommies and other ladies in the know flock here for everything a woman needs to keep her sex life interesting.

Whether you're heading for one of the city's dungeons or wild swingers parties, or you just want to surprise your unsuspecting boyfriend back home, these are the best places to pick up the naughty items that will have airport security doing double-takes!

PURPLE PASSION

211 W 20TH ST
212 807 0486
23RD ST STATION
WWW.PURPLEPASSION.COM

This lovely lavender store is the place to go for all things S/M Fetish. Whether you're looking for leather, latex or PVC, you'll find it here, along with a selection of over 300 corsets. The store also stocks boots and shoes — the sort that will make you look very commanding in the bedroom! Petite to plus-sizes means there's something to fit dominatrixes-in-training of any size or shape.

THE LEATHER MAN

111 CHRISTOPHER ST
212 243 5339
CHRISTOPHER ST STATION
WWW.THELEATHERMAN.COM

This store is definitely not for those who consider themselves "vanilla." Although their customers are mostly gay men, all flavors are welcome here, with a nice selection of women's leather clothing and boots. If you're into an alternative lifestyle, it's the best place to pick up new items for your arsenal. Downstairs you'll find floggers, paddles, collars and all the other accoutrement you'll need to bring out your inner dominatrix.

THE BARONESS

530B E 13TH ST
212 529 5964
14TH ST STATION
WWW.BARONESS.COM

Whether you're looking for a lipstick red latex jacket, a custom made black corset or a purple cincher belt, The Baroness is here to serve you. Her alternative rubber fetish fashions may look clingy but are actually quite comfortable. Dresses, pants and skirts come in a variety of exotic colors from lime green to pale pink and you can get anything custom-made. And for the wannabe Matrix man in your life, The Baroness also does menswear.

TRASH & VAUDEVILLE

4 SAINT MARKS PLACE
212 982 3590
ASTOR PLACE STATION

If you're looking to revisit your punk rock roots, find your inner Goth girl or just ramp up your look from sexy to so-hot-it-hurts, T&V has got you covered. This unique East Village staple is actually two stores — the kitschy, brightly-colored Vaudeville is upstairs while the more hardcore Trash resides below street level. While some complain that the prices are high, most agree that so is the quality of the items you'll find here.

EROTIC EDUCATION

"Ready to become more sensual?"

E ven the sexiest and most confident women know there's always something new and exciting to learn when it comes to sex. And there's no better place to get schooled in the sensual arts than right here in New York City. In a place that thrives on ambition, self development, and freedom – especially of the sexual persuasion – you'll find experts, educators, coaches, and communities sharing advice and tips on everything from tantric sex and pleasure coaching to pole dancing and how to transform yourself into a Pin-Up glamour girl. Savvy travelers won't pass up the opportunity to take advantage of these amazing resources. And the wisdom and talents you bring home won't even take up any space in your suitcase.

LOVERS

COMPILED BY

Mary

India Sinha

tantra

THE ROMANTIC FLOWER

The Art of Tantric Romance

CLAUDE MAZLO

The Amorous Man

A History of Erot

A History of Ero

A History of Er

SEXY SPIRITS
WWW.SEXYSPIRITS.COM/BLOG

Forget the gimmicks and misguided advice of Cosmo and
other "women's" magazines. Sexy Spirits aims to be a sex-
positive, supportive community where men and women
"honor, understand, and celebrate our sexual nature."
There's a full schedule of events and classes on topics such
as Women & Power, Sacred Sexuality, Sensual Love &
Intimacy, Orgasmic Meditation, and even online courses in
Tantric Massage and Sexual Energy.

TANTRIC SEX
WWW.TANTRAPM.COM

Married couple Mark A. Michaels (Swami Umeshanand
Saraswati) and Patricia Johnson (Devi Veenanand) teach
the art of Tantra to both couples and singles. Learn to
recognize specific zones of the body that are responsive
to stimulation and extend the excitement phase of sex.
Their goal is to help students bring an expanded capac-
ity for pleasure into everyday life.

PERSONAL SEX COACHING
TEL 866 877 9676
WWW.DODSONANDROSS.COM

Sexologist Betty Dodson provides sex coaching for
women and couples at her studio in Midtown. For
women who struggle with reaching orgasm, or who
just want to improve their sexual skills, her tutelage
is a godsend. With decades of practice and a hands-on
approach, Betty knows how to make her clients feel at
ease in order to help them reach their sexual potential.

ONE TASTE
WWW.ONETASTE.US
800 994 0041

Ready to Become More Sensual? Explore the philosophy
behind OneTaste, a place that teaches
Slow Sex and Orgasmic Meditation. Get out of your
head and into your body with their workshops, lectures
and free meetups.

"Is sex dirty? Only if it's done right" —WOODY ALLEN

NEW YORK SCHOOL OF BURLESQUE

440 LAFAYETTE
TEL 212 561 1456
EMAIL ROCKNYCITY@AOL.COM
WWW.SCHOOLOFBURLESQUE.COM

Headmistress Jo Weldon helps ladies of all shapes and sizes discover their confidence and develop stage personas through Thursday night burlesque classes. Learn the language of burlesque and movement, pick a burlesque name and spend time developing your routine. Jo teaches fan dancing, chair dancing and boa play, and unlike regular striptease, the routines follow a narrative and incorporate costumes, humor and just about anything else you can imagine.

"To dance is to be out of yourself. Larger, more beautiful, more powerful."

—AGNES DE MILLE

PIN-UP FINISHING SCHOOL

WWW.PINUPFINISHINGSCHOOL.COM

Day-long Pin-Up classes where burlesque performer and Pin-Up model Rocket J shares her tips on beauty, posing, wardrobe and having fun with props. Each participant leaves with an 8x10 print of her favorite pose (from $250). There are also hands-on Hair Seminars where you learn how to create those great retro styles (from $75).

GO-GO AMY

WWW.GOGOAMY.COM

Pin-Up model and burlesque dancer Go-Go Amy conducts monthly Pin-Up Girl classes for both seasoned models and absolute beginners. Amy insists that true glamour has no height, size or age requirement. "All you need is a positive attitude and an open mind." All participants get a CD of photos and a goody bag at the end of the session. From $200.

Luscious Lifestyle Diva

347 497 DIVA
WWW.LUSCIOUSLIFESTYLEDIVA.COM

Media personality, courtesan coach, and lifestyle expert Yolanda Shoshana brings back the virtues – and pleasures – of the courtesans in her modern day courtesan school. Learn the art of seduction, tap into your charm, talents, wit, beauty, and grace. She provides one-on-one or group coaching and workshops, aphrodisiac cooking classes and courtesan crawls. Her goal is to help women tap into their inner courtesan to live a luscious life.

Tied Up Events

WWW.TIEDUPEVENTS.COM

Interested in learning more about the art of bondage? Dee "Diva" Dennis and Tess Danesi host several events and educational conferences throughout the year featuring internationally acclaimed bondage artists and other sex educators and personalities. They also publish the Sex Bloggers Calendar for sex-positive charities.

S Factor

235 WEST 23RD STREET AND 147 WEST 24TH STREET
23RD STREET STATION
212 989 8030
WWW.SFACTOR.COM

What do you get when you combine sexy pole dance moves with a thorough body workout and a supportive, female-focused environment? Nothing less than S Factor, created by former ballet dancer Sheila Kelley. More than just a swivel around a pole, S Factor is about "Helping women become comfortable with, able to express and own their wholesome sexuality." There are pole dancing, lap dancing, and fitness components to the lessons. Discover new, sensual ways to move your body.

Exotic Dance Central

12 E. 32ND ST
MURRAY HILL, 33RD ST STATION
212 679 2540
WWW.EXOTICDANCECENTRAL.COM

Beginners are welcome to take a spin on the pole at Exotic Dance Central. Learn a new art form while breaking a sweat in this step by step pole dancing program including strengthening exercises, poses and, of course, spins. Advance to pole tricks when you're ready. Note: Rest assured – there are no spectators permitted here and absolutely no nudity.

FOR THEM OR FOR YOU

WWW.FORTHEMORFORYOU.COM
914 466 4347

Pin-Up Girl Workshops with photographer Charise Isis where participants get a vintage makeover, access to Isis's collection of costumes and props, and playful instruction on how to bring out your sensuality and sex it up for the camera. The class ends with group and individual portrait sessions. Ready for your close up? From $250 per person; private boudoir sessions from $500.

SHAMELESS

WWW.SHAMELESSPHOTO.COM
646 448 8227

Let photographer, make-up artist and hair stylist Sophie Spinelle transform you into a Pin-Up Goddess. Ready with all the necessary wardrobe, props and accessories, her goal is to capture women at their most confident and beautiful, even if they've never posed before. Packages from $250 for small groups, $395 for individuals.

COUTURE BOUDOIR

WWW.COUTUREBOUDOIR.COM

Critsey Rowe is an internationally acclaimed wedding and boudoir photographer whose images have been published in popular magazines around the world. With the help of hair and make-up stylists, she aims to capture each woman's own intimate beauty. These high-quality fashion portraits are then transformed into prints that will last a lifetime. Packages from $800.

"There's a side of my personality that goes completely against the East Coast educated person and wants to be a pin-up girl in garages across America...there's a side that wants to wear the pink angora bikini!"
—ACTRESS MIRA SORVINO

PART V

New York Nights

DRINKING

> *"Why don't you slip out of those wet clothes and into a dry Martini?"* —ROBERT BENCHLEY

It's not that we think you should get naked (right away). But as fuel for fun, we definitely recommend getting a drink. In moderation, booze is liquid flirtation, or lust on the rocks. And New York City is definitely a place where enjoying it is a state-of-the-art experience. With small-batch distilleries popping up around the world, there is more to choose from in the spirits realm—and New York's increasing pool of quality mixologists are taking advantage. The bounty's not limited to cocktails, either: the heightened awareness about good drinks has raised the bar (pun intended) overall. Fine, heady wines are available everywhere and rich craft brews such as Brooklyn lager and Sixpoint Sweet Action are both made right here in New York. The city's newfound lust for well-made alcohol has boosted its bar count—particularly in the realm of spots beloved by ladies. And why wouldn't we love them? The new bars are classy and playful, beautiful and naughty, and either wickedly secret or wildly ostentatious.

ASPEN SOCIAL CLUB

157 W. 47TH STREET
212 221 7200
49TH STREET STATION
WWW.ASPENSOCIALCLUB.COM

Finally, Times Square has a restaurant bar that's strong enough for a man…but ideal for a woman. At the Aspen Social Club you leave the flashing neon streets behind and step into a swanky ski lodge of rough-hewn wood planks, antlers, leather booths and low-lit nooks, perfect for naughty make-out sessions with one of the handsome young bankers who frequent the bar early in the evening. The drink list is long, with cocktails like the rose-hued Açai Margarita and Vesper Martinis available by the glass ($14) or pitcher ($60). The crowd gets younger after 10pm when tables are cleared for dancing. Bottle service on weekends (starts at $175) guarantees a table. But for women? Bring a pack of your girlfriends, smile sweetly, and enjoy this midtown treehouse.
Hours: Tue-Thurs 7am-2am; Fri-Sat 7am-4am. Reservations recommended.

LE BAIN

THE STANDARD HOTEL, 18TH FLOOR
848 WASHINGTON STREET
212 645 4646
8TH AVENUE STATION
WWW.STANDARDHOTELS.COM/NEW-YORK-CITY

Don't bother checking the website. The bars crowning the edgy Standard Hotel are so hot they need no introduction. If you're young and smokin', or can carry off a "look" with confidence, head up to Le Bain. The bi-level bar features faux grass, kitschy lounge chairs, cocktails from $16, an enormous hot tub (in season) and stunning rooftop views over the city. After 11pm it has more of a club vibe. If you're one of the lucky few, you may get invited to mingle with the A-list at the even more exclusive Boom Boom Room next door. Its view of the Hudson, the massive, high-ceilinged prow-shaped room and plush banquettes makes you feel as if you've left Manhattan, and walked onto a glamorous cruise liner. **Open: Mon-Wed 10pm-4am; Thu-Sun noon-4am.**

BLUE RUIN

538 9TH AVENUE
917 945 3497
42ND ST/PORT AUTHORITY STATION

This anything-goes dive bar takes a page from Hogs & Heifers — sans the tiresome script. What this means: to the delight of a widely eclectic clientele, all of its bartenders are ballsy women with random tendencies to holler, dance on the bar, and blow big balls of fire. Named after spoiled bathtub gin, the vibe is worn-in Americana, from the gas lamp lighting to the pine plank flooring. Drinks-wise, the selections don't veer far from basic beers, Jaegar shots to be pounded hastily, and sickly sweet cocktails. Drinks, of course, are sort of beside the point. This is a place to come kick off your shoes, climb onto a bar (women only), and join a chorus of raucous bachelorettes to an ACDC sing-a-long. **Open Mon-Sat 11am-4am; Sun from noon.**

THE BUNKER CLUB

24 9TH AVENUE
212 837 4700
14TH STREET STATION
WWW.BUNKERCLUBNYC.COM

A word of warning: You'll fall in love at least twice here—once with the adorable bartenders donning khaki threads, and a second time with the boys getting drinks from them. Best described as "wartime chic," this subterranean MPD spot 30 feet below a casual burger joint is where you'd want to be should an air raid ever strike. A long bar faces low seating for groups and a D.J. booth overlooks the black-and-white tiled dance floor. And if this place seems familiar, it is—it's the same owner as the beloved (and now defunct) Beatrice Inn where you undoubtedly spent many nights underneath the disco ball. (Look up, that disco ball's still here.) Sip a beer or G&T and get that old familiar feeling, even if it's your first visit.

KASTEL

TRUMP SOHO
246 SPRING STREET
212 842 5500
SPRING STREET STATION
WWW.TRUMPSOHOHOTEL.COM

If you're looking for a place to put your money where your mouth is, then head to hotel hotspot Kastel. Who else can provide Fendi furniture to go with your Fendi Peekaboo bag? Only a Trump, of course. Inside his latest nighttime destination, PYTs (pretty young things) converse with moneyed men over $18 Trump Vodka cocktails, so choose wisely. Unlike the staid reputation of his other properties, the Donald sexes up this scene with chain-mail curtains, leather banquettes and scattered velvet ottomans while a DJ spins high above the seating area. Crowds are easy to get in before 10pm, but after that a door policy is in effect with a separate entrance on Varick Street. Open nightly, 4pm-2am.

LUCKY DOG

303 BEDFORD AVE
BROOKLYN, BEDFORD AVENUE STATION

We once brought a date here, a preppy trader from Manhattan. He took a perplexed look around, and said, "It looks like everyone has just come in from chopping wood." We couldn't have put it better. At this dog-friendly pub, cute beerheads don trim beards, plaid, and ironic glasses, and down good local craft beer with Pink Floyd and the White Stripes blaring (when crowded, don't even attempt the jukebox rotation). People (mostly men) arrive in 3s and 4s, and the über-friendly vibe – and Williamsburg in general – guarantee an absence of attitude. Inside, there's an ongoing game of pick-up shuffleboard (we always offer to play winners, then get a cute guy to "teach" us). Outdoors are communal tables and a fire pit. **Open Mon-Fri 2pm-4am; Sat-Sun from noon.**

APOTHÉKE

9 DOYERS STREET
212 406 0400
CANAL STREET STATION
WWW.APOTHEKEBAR.COM

Not only did *Romeo & Juliet* immortalize the great European apothecary, it also bestowed Old World medicinal shops with a (fatal) sex appeal. Rather than kill you, Apothéke's "prescriptions" first work on revving you up and tickling your libido. The Chinatown bar and its handsomely bespectacled, lab-coated "chemists" make extensive use of elixirs and infusions such as pine vodka, lavender gin, habañero tequila. But really, this former opium den is not so much a cocktail parlor as a public aphrodisiac. The journey there requires a stroll down a once-scary alley (the "Bloody Angle"), then through a *chop suey* restaurant. Behind the heavy velvet curtain you'll find an intricate tin ceiling, Victorian sofas and a glimmering marble bar. The perfect backdrop for a smoldering glance, or six.
 Open daily 6:30pm-2am, Sun from 8pm.

THE BAR DOWNSTAIRS

ANDAZ 5TH AVENUE
485 5TH AVENUE
212 601 1234
BRYANT PARK STATION
WWW.ANDAZ5THAVENUE.COM

You know that friend who entertains like she travels, with class and panache? Step into her home at this subterranean bar. Like an elegant underground lodge, this cozy drink spot mixes rich walnut slabs with contemporary cylindrical lights, perfect for rubbing knees with the list of posh clientele that frequents this place. On the menu? Try the signature drink, The Cellar Door that mixes Pimms #1, bergamot syrup, lemon and spiced rum to create a sensory sip. If you don't think it goes perfectly with a plate of locally sourced cheeses and other farm fresh eats, rest assured it will look divine next to your Goyard clutch.
Open Mon-Sat, 5:00pm-12:00am.

COVET

137 EAST 55TH STREET
212 223 2829
53RD STREET STATION

If working late means more than filing that report, this oversized lounge with a strategic midtown location is your place for undercover trysts. Don't let the modest exterior fool you: inside the bi-level space, dark wood seats and fur throws create an ambiance that would make anyone giddy for a good time. Filled with the perfect blend of financial types and newly minted moguls looking for their next prey, the crowd here is Wall Street meets The Devil Wears Prada. Sit pretty with your ladies and sip a Cupid (vodka infused with dill and habañero bitters), or the Shaman Colada, made with Hungarian paprika and precooked pineapple Mezcal. And after you get warmed up? Hit the hidden lover's den in the back, complete with a bed and mirrored ceilings. **Open Mon-Sat 5:30pm-4am.**

LANI KAI

525 BROOME STREET
646 596 8778
SPRING STREET STATION
WWW.LANIKAINY.COM

A decidedly modern spin on your traditional tiki bar, the only sighting of palm trees is on the wallpaper downstairs at Lani Kai. More hang ten than haughty, a gas fireplace replaces a fire pit and plastic trees get a grown up treatment with an installation of lush tropical plants. But those looking for Zombies and Scorpion bowls might want to head to more kitschy spots—cool cocktails like The Lone Palm, Hotel California and Pacific Swizzle are adorned with grilled pineapple or orchid flowers. But tiki is as tiki does, so if you're really down to party, try a liquid luau (large cocktails meant for sharing ($52-$65) and wash it down with noteworthy Asian-tinged bites. Open daily 5pm-2am, Fri-Sat until 3am.

FLÛTE

40 E. 20TH STREET
212 529 7870
23RD ST/LEXINGTON STATION
WWW.FLUTEBAR.COM

There isn't another bar on our list that's so hell-bent on one thing: popping your cork. Luckily, we like ours popped... often, and emphatically! So we come to Flute. Even bubbles need somewhere to float or land, and Flute provides that. The bar is the second incarnation of owner Hervé Rousseau's lifelong obsession with brut. On DJ nights, it's like a candlelit nook in a smoldering French nightclub: couples make out on deep settees, while groups and newer dates cavort at the bar and in the cozy indoor cabana. As for the bubbles themselves, Flute has an impressive range: big and little; straight and mixed; French and faux; pink, white, even red. Everything that sparkles is here, from a long list of Champagne cocktails, to sparkling Shiraz and sake. **Open Sun-Wed 4pm-2am; Thurs 4pm-3am; Fri, Sat 4pm-4am.**

MAYAHUEL

304 E 6TH STREET
212 253 5888
ASTOR PL/8TH ST/LEXINGTON STATION
WWW.MAYAHUELNY.COM

According to legend, the agave plant sprouted from the body of the slain Aztec goddess Mayahuel. A fitting name for this erotically-charged Mexican restaurant and bar specializing in the finest tequilas and Mezcals. Downstairs, things are darkly brooding, with a carved wood bar and rafters, intimate booths and whimsical mariachi figurines. Upstairs, the blue velvet banquettes enjoy plunging curves ("they call this the baby-making room," says owner Ravi DeRossi). Small wonder we love coming here with our dates, leaning back and gazing up at the giant red jewel of a tarantula (which spawns inside agave plants) on the ceiling, or through the sexy mesh peekaboo to the bar beneath. Forget lemon, salt, or chasers and instead opt for tequila cocktails or punch, paired with a delicate plate of food such as the sweet plantains. **Open Mon-Sat 6pm-2am; Sun 2pm-midnight.**

ROSE & JADE BAR

GRAMERCY PARK HOTEL
2 LEXINGTON AVENUE
212 920 3300
23RD ST/LEXINGTON STATION
WWW.GRAMERCYPARKHOTEL.COM

It's hard not to feel indulgently spoiled in this artsy cocoon. The vibe—crackling hearth, textured interiors—is hot. The drinks ($19 and up)—Diamond and Pearls (vodka, muddled blackberries, coconut syrup), rose & litchi martinis—are sexy. Skin—on the lovely barmaids, the lovely patrons—is in evidence. And the surroundings are astoundingly tasteful. Small wonder: the designer Julian Schnabel, not only an eye for what works, he also crafted much of the furniture himself, and provided his own paintings to hang alongside those of Andy Warhol, Jean-Michel Basquiat, Damien Hirst, and Keith Haring. The Jade is a slice of bar – open to the public. The Rose is tougher – ask your concierge to get you on the list. Once you're in, try to stare at the artwork, not the A-list clientele. **Open noon-4am.**

TOP OF THE STRAND

33 W 37TH STREET
212 448 1024
34TH ST/HERALD SQUARE STATION
WWW.THESTRANDNYC.COM

Unlike Manhattan's other roof bars, Top of the Strand requires no heat lamps, blankets, or house robes. A massive, retractable glass roof stays closed in winter, keeping things snowflake-proof (but still visible), and slides open when things warm up to let in the breeze—and sounds—of the city. Just three blocks away, the Empire State Building looms so big we can see its reflection in our cocktails. Come here with friends to mingle in the intimate space with the fashion-, media-, theater-savvy crowd. As for drinks, the four-section cocktail menu was made for women. Pluck a Cosmopolitan off the "Modern" list, a Mint Julep off the "Classic" list, a sweetly heady Singapore Sling off the "Exotic List"…the alcohol content can vary, but the good cheer will not. **Open 5pm-midnight, Fri-Sat until 1am.**

BRANDY LIBRARY

25 N MOORE STREET
212 226 5545
FRANKLIN STREET STATION
WWW.BRANDYLIBRARY.COM

If we feel a yen to visit a gentleman's club, we snare our girlfriends (no more than six) and head straight for this elegant Tribeca bar. With its leather seats, mahogany shelving, silk-clad "librarians" (servers), and hushed vibe, the Brandy Library looks like, sounds like, and stocks like a men-only establishment, except for one small fact: the clientele actually skews 60-40 in favor of women like us. "Women are way more adventurous about trying new drinks," says debonair French founder Flavien Desoblin, adding that men too often "just want their Macallan." With over 900 brandies, cognacs, rums, whiskeys, bourbons, ryes, tequilas, Mezcals, and Scotches we love to flex our adventurous palates, while ogling the toughest of Wall Street' lingering banker crowd. **Open Sun-Wed, 5pm to 1am; Thurs 4pm-2am; Fri-Sat 4pm-4am. Reservations strongly advised.**

"I like to have a Martini, two at the very most; three,
I'm under the table, four I'm under my host!"
—DOROTHY PARKER

BRANDY LIBRARY

JIMMY

JAMES HOTEL
15 THOMPSON STREET
212 465 2000
CANAL STREET STATION
WWW.JIMMYSOHO.COM

More 1970's moody than Miami with its herringbone floors and leather-trimmed solid wood bar, Jimmy offers stunning 360-degree views over the Manhattan skyline. During summer, stretch out by the pool on teak chaises while sipping on a Chanel No.9, nine floral and botanical liquors blended with champagne. But don't let cold weather steer you away— come winter, indoor seating and fireplaces beckon you upstairs to enjoy a creation by pro mixologists. **Open 5pm-1am, Mon-Wed. Thurs-Sat until 2am.**

BAR PLEIADES

THE SURREY HOTEL
20 EAST 76TH STREET
212 288 3700
77TH STREET STATION
WWW.THESURREY.COM

Looking for cool cocktails in a chic setting? With a nod to Chanel—black-and-white lacquered tables and plush white couches—this spot creates a sexy scene perfect for checking out the pin-striped regulars. Try the Capsicum Cooler that has aquavit, gin and lemon bitters, or the Beijing Mule with Asian pear vodka and house fermented ginger beer. And while you won't be dancing on the banquettes, give the boys in their three-piece suits a chance to loosen their ties before calling it a night. **Open daily, 12pm-12am.**

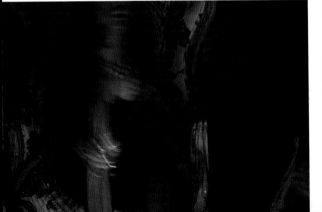

LILLIE'S

13 E 17TH STREET
212 337 1970
UNION SQUARE/14TH ST STATION
WWW.LILLIESNYC.COM

A bay window and landmark doors lead the way to this Irish-Victorian saloon, a boisterous tribute to turn-of-the-century vaudeville actress Lillie Langtry. During sporting events, both genders pile in to watch on flat screens, with long flutes of Prosecco, stylish selves perched on red velvet banquettes. But with an ornate 56' marble bar, stained glass windows, mismatched chandeliers, and Victorian paintings, this is one elegant sports bar. A second location can be found in Times Square. **Open daily 11am-4am.**

ECC LOWER EAST SIDE

191 CHRYSTIE STREET
BOWERY STATION
WWW.EXPERIMENTALCOCKTAILCLUBNY.COM

Four years ago, three young Frenchmen inspired by New York City's underground cocktail bars took the idea across the Atlantic, creating four of the most popular bars in Paris and one in London. Now the Experimental Cocktail Club is taking on Manhattan's Lower East Side...with a French Touch! Enjoy a vast selection of spirits and vintage Cognacs around the grand piano and oversized fireplace, or grab a breath of fresh air in the *jardin d'hiver.* **Open daily, 6pm-4am.**

TERROIR
413 E 12TH STREET
212 602 1300
1ST AVE/14TH ST STATION
WWW.WINEISTERROIR.COM

Wine lovers adore this East Village icon: a fun-loving, easy-going wine bar that doesn't take itself too seriously…but has serious wines. The wine list reads like a magazine with random pop culture commentaries (one entry compares a favorite winemaker with Britney Spears). and light, amusing remarks about the wines (including the expected Rieslings and Burgundies, and the unexpected Mexican wines, beers, and ciders), their makers, and, true to the bar's name, their terroir. The bartender is friendly. The vibe is romantic. The food (cured meats, cheeses, paninis) is delicious. No one pulls airs. The only hard part is getting in, with just 24 stools and no room to spare. The bar or communal table are both good bets, and it's well worth the wait. **Open Sun-Wed 5pm-1am; Thurs 4pm-2am, Fri-Sat 4pm-4am.**

BYOB

Looking for a parlor party far away from scene? Head back to the 1930s at this consummate jazz venue located in the building that hosted Billie Holiday's first gigs. The locals will tell you they want to keep this cool cat spot a secret, but owner Bill Saxton (a jazz saxophonist extraordinaire and a Harlem legend) will lure you into the first floor of this brownstone with his groovy beats. It's a no frills place that doesn't serve alcohol, but Bill encourages the convivial spirit by allowing you to bring in your own bottle. Set in a warm, rich atmosphere, the experience is intimate, inviting and one that can't be missed if you're a jazz fan. But there aren't many seats available, so reservations are a must. Open Fridays, 10pm and midnight. $15 per performance. Saturdays, special performances. $20. Bill's Place (148 West 133rd Street, tel 212 281 0777, 135th Street station, www.billsaxton.com).

Beware

Many bars now stamping 18-20% gratuity onto the bill "because of European guests who don't tip". Don't make the mistake of tipping on top of this!

MANHATTAN
DINING

> *"For many New Yorkers, a date is the perfect excuse to try a new restaurant."*

Lingering glances over Pinot Noir. Probing stares over diver scallops. When it comes to Manhattan's dining scene, flirtation is the name of the game. And you need only walk into a restaurant bar for that game to begin. Don't be surprised if you notice locals giving you the once over – in New York, every attractive stranger holds the promise of romantic adventure.

"In general, I think, human beings are happiest at a table when they are very young, very much in love or very alone." —FOOD CRITIC MARY FRANCES KENNEDY FISHER

Solo Dining

Dining alone tonight? Not for long. Ordering a meal at the bar of any of these restaurants will ensure that you'll want for neither company nor entertainment. After all, if you'd really wanted to eat alone, you could have just ordered room service.

THE SPOTTED PIG

314 WEST 11TH ST, AT GREENWICH ST
212 620 0393
WEST VILLAGE, CHRISTOPHER ST STATION
WWW.THESPOTTEDPIG.COM

The Spotted Pig's warm ambiance and consistent seasonal fare draw people from every point of the spectrum. Having pioneered the British gastropub trend, the Pig is both a foodie's dream and a single girl's best friend. A seat at the bar virtually guarantees you both an unforgettable meal (deviled eggs, chicken liver toasts, gnudi and the burger are favorites) and an equally memorable conversation. Dinner $25 - $60.

THE BALTHAZAR

80 SPRING ST, AT CROSBY ST
212 965 1414
SOHO, SPRING ST STATION
WWW.BALTHAZARNY.COM

The ultimate "it" restaurant, the famous Balthazar has been a hit with locals and tourists alike since the day it first elevated the bread basket, Steak Frites and Nicoise Salad to an art form in 1997. The bar at this perpetually booked resto is where the real action happens. Fashionistas and models mingle with starchitects and Internet millionaires. Very chic, very smart and very naughty. Dinner $30-$65.

CASIMIR

103 AVENUE B
212 358 9683
EAST VILLAGE, ASTOR PLACE STATION
WWW.CASIMIRRESTAURANT.COM

Looking for something more laid back? Then leave your bandage dress in the closet and head to Casimir in the East Village. A low-key French bistro with a Moroccan flair and some pronounced Eastern European influences (herring and potatoes, anyone?), Casimir is a favorite with hip, young locals who like a little people-watching with their oysters. No lipstick required, but you will need your Amex. Dinner $25-$45.

EXTRA VIRGIN

259 WEST 4TH ST
212 691 9359
WEST VILLAGE, CHRISTOPHER ST STATION
WWW.EXTRAVIRGINRESTAURANT.COM

From the ultra hip to the world famous, the crowd at this sophisticated Italian establishment appreciates a laid-back atmosphere and well-edited menu. The bartenders will make you feel at home. And if you play your cards right, maybe one of the cute guys hanging out by the bar will offer to subsidize your next dirty martini. Dinner $30-$55.

PASTIS

9 NINTH AVE, AT LITTLE WEST 12TH ST
212 929 4844
MEATPACKING DISTRICT, 8TH AVE/14 TH ST STATION
WWW.PASTISNY.COM

There's a reason Pastis was such a favorite on Sex and the City. As the Meatpacking District's flagship restaurant, the vibe at this glitzy, French brasserie is fun, festive and friendly. The bar fills up with revelers come happy hour and doesn't ease up until well into the wee hours with married, single and single-for-the-night gents in Varvatos suits and ladies in Louboutins. Dinner $30-$60.

Dinner for Two

For many New Yorkers, a date is the perfect excuse to try a new restaurant. And that goes double for couples in from out of town. Feeding each other dessert over candlelight, playing footsie while pretending to listen to the specials...now that's what we call romantic. You've got the partner in crime, now all you need is the right venue to set the stage for an intimate night full of laughter, romance and who knows what else.

BLUE RIBBON DOWNING STREET BAR

34 DOWNING ST
212 691 0404
WEST VILLAGE, HOUSTON ST STATION
WWW.BLUERIBBONRESTAURANTS.COM

Dimly lit and densely populated, this tiny West Village charmer will leave you no choice but to get a little closer. While you won't find any tables here, just bar-seating, you will be delighted by the wine list, wooed by the oyster shooters and thoroughly seduced by some of the best steak tartare in the city (if not the universe). Wine $8-18, Dinner $25 - $55.

PER SE

10 COLUMBUS CIRCLE, TIME WARNER CENTER, 4TH FLOOR
UPPER WEST SIDE, 59TH ST/COLUMBUS CIRCLE STATION
212 823 9335
WWW.PERSENY.COM

You wanted the best-in-class? If you're turned on by the prospect of a multi-course meal at what is arguably the best French restaurant in the country then you'll feel downright feverish at Thomas Keller's Per Se. Overlooking Central Park, this elegant dining room beckons you to relinquish control and indulge your appetites. Share this once-in-a-lifetime meal with someone special, because this is one dinner you'll never want to forget. Wine $20-$36, Tasting Menu $275.

LA ESQUINA

106 KENMARE STREET
SOHO, SPRING ST STATION
646 613 7100
WWW.ESQUINANY.COM

Don't worry about being in the wrong place, the taco stand is only a front. Get past the door guard, descend down the stairs, walk through a busy kitchen, and lo and behold, a dark, cavernous lounge awaits. Start at the bar with margaritas or go straight for the fish tacos and the corn on the cob (so worth it, but bring dental floss) and save the mingling for later. Dinner $35-$60.

BREAKFAST

La Esquina

SUSHI YASUDA

204 EAST 43RD ST
212 972 1001
MIDTOWN EAST, GRAND CENTRAL STATION
WWW.SUSHIYASUDA.COM

Warning: The only scene you're likely to find at this sushi purist's paradise is a lot of people looking very serious about every tantalizing morsel that passes their lips. Reserve two seats at the bar, preferably in front of Chef Yasuda himself, then relax and let the maestro take care of the rest. A never-ending series of delectables, Yasuda's refreshing omakasae is the perfect prelude to a scorching night. Dinner $175.

JEAN GEORGES

1 CENTRAL PARK WEST
212 299 3900
UPPER WEST SIDE, 59TH ST/COLUMBUS CIRCLE STATION

If a long and decadent meal is your idea of foreplay, then Jean Georges will get you in the mood. Formal without being stuffy, this bastion of the city's finest culinary talent plays host to corporate raiders, media moguls and haute cuisine lovers. If you're looking for a dinner worthy of your passion (to say nothing of your best Chanel), you got it. For a less formal setting, try Nougatine next door. Tasting Menu $98.

CASA LA FEMME

140 CHARLES STREET
212 505 0005
WEST VILLAGE, CHRISTOPHER ST STATION
WWW.CASALAFEMMENY.COM

Belly dancers, hookahs and private tents? You're three for three at New York's premier date spot. The exotic Casa La Femme brings the sensual spirit and authentic cuisine of Alexandria to the West Village, transporting you and your lucky consort into a gilded fantasy straight out of 1001 Arabian Nights. And while the tagines are certainly delicious, it's the ambiance that will be to blame for your semi-public display of affection (people can see into those tents, you know). Dinner $50-$75

LITTLE GIANT

85 ORCHARD STREET
212 226 5047
LOWER EAST SIDE, ESSEX ST/DELANCEY ST STATION
WWW.LITTLEGIANTNYC.COM

If your tastes run towards the understated, you can't miss this cozy little dining room on the Lower East Side. Wooden tables, dim lighting and hearty, seasonal American fare conspire to create a rustic, farmhouse feel, enticing couples to steal off for the haystacks after dinner. Dinner $35-$65.

Girls Night Out

There's nothing like a night out with the girls in a town where everyone is always looking for the next best thing and living for the moment. Here, every restaurant is crammed with revelers and roving eyes looking to make that love connection. Bring your finest wingwomen and don't look so shocked when the gentlemen at the neighboring table casually engage you in witty banter.

INDOCHINE

430 LAFAYETTE ST
212 505 5111
EAST VILLAGE, ASTOR PLACE STATION
WWW.INDOCHINENYC.COM

More than 25 years after its debut, this ultra sexy French-Vietnamese restaurant has lost none of its allure. From the varied menu to the preponderance of potted palms, everything at Indochine aims to please and entice – including the stunning hostesses and male servers. The clientele ranges from die hard traditionalists who have been coming since the 80s to nouveau rockers. Ask to be seated at one of the brown leather banquette tables. Dinner $45-$60.

THE STANDARD GRILL

848 WASHINGTON STREET
MEATPACKING DISTRICT, 8TH AVENUE STATION
212 645 4100
WWW.THESTANDARDGRILL.COM

The sight of so many well-dressed men crowding the Standard's bright, whitewashed bar area is just the beginning of the fun. This hotel resto is happening every night of the week, so reserve a table in the bar area and have yourselves a feast as you watch the show and decide whom you'll approach after you've polished off your duck fat smashed potatoes. Dinner $45-$70

PRAVDA

281 LAFAYETTE STREET
SOHO, SPRING ST STATION
212 226 4696
WWW.PRAVDANY.COM

Whether or not you've got a fascination with the former
Soviet Union, you'll find plenty to hold your interest at
this subterranean speakeasy styled after a Russian bath-
house. Even the menu doesn't strain the motif, offering
well-chosen selections like smoked fish and caviar blini,
yet still including international faves like calamari.
Dinner $40–$190 if you spring for the Sevruga.

MINETTA TAVERN

113 MACDOUGAL STREET
WEST VILLAGE, WEST 4TH ST STATION
212 475 3850
WWW.MINETTATAVERNNY.COM

New York's well-heeled and well-connected frequent
the city's most buzzed about new restaurant, regularly
drawing the likes of Madonna, the Clintons and Anna
Wintour to its well guarded doorstep. Reputed to
have the best burger in Manhattan and a decor that is a
cross between French steakhouse and grandpa's library,
Minetta Tavern is also a great place to hunt for it all,
from a hook-up to a husband. Dinner $50–$90.

FREEMANS

END OF FREEMAN ALLEY, OFF RIVINGTON
LOWER EAST SIDE, 2ND AVE/LOWER EAST SIDE STATION
212 420 0012
WWW.FREEMANSRESTAURANT.COM

Plaid shirts, ironic facial hair, skinny jeans – Freemans
has been a magnet for the city's artsy types with its
rustic American cuisine and taxidermy-rich decor. The
hard-to-find location at the end of tiny Freeman Alley
is as much of a draw as the restaurant's famous Hot
Artichoke Dip and Devils on Horseback appetizers.
There's a no-reservations policy (parties under six), so
grab a cocktail and hang out. Dinner $40–$65.

CRAFT

43 EAST 19TH ST
212 780 0880
FLATIRON, 23RD ST STATION
WWW.CRAFTRESTAURANT.COM

The crown jewel of Tom Colicchio's empire is a clean, airy, well-lit space that radiates chic sophistication from every one of the innumerable filament bulbs that hang brightly from its ceiling. This is a dinner date crowd, so you and your companion should feel right at home as you lock eyes and swoon over every delicious bite. Cocktails $14, Dinner $50-$85

Celebriquette

Ooh! There's Jude Law! Omg! That's Natalie Portman. Wait a second! Is that Counting Crows lead singer Adam Durvitz? All of these thoughts and questions are to be whispered discreetly among your friends as you do your best to appear as though you're talking about something completely unrelated to the celebrity. Prolonged staring, any attempts to befriend the celebrity or even just engage him or her in conversation are strictly prohibited in Manhattan's finer restaurants. And don't even think about autograph requests.

THE BRESLIN

16 WEST 29TH STREET
FLATIRON, 28TH ST STATION
212 679 1939
WWW.THEBRESLIN.COM

Even in a town the size of Manhattan, there are only ever a few really hot restaurants. At the moment, the Breslin is one of these. Ace Hotel's restaurant is a wood-paneled den of British gastro-grub. Start with rustic, farmhouse decor, throw in some Scotch Eggs and Beef and Stilton Pie, then finish off with hipsters in Prohibition-era dress, and you've got yourself a party. Dinner $55-$75.

MORANDI

211 WAVERLY PLACE
212 627 7575
WEST VILLAGE, CHRISTOPHER ST
WWW.MORANDINY.COM

You'll see plenty of the city's most eligible bachelors circulating through this rustic Italian trattoria. A magnet for the city's young, rich and famous, Morandi boasts a substantial bar area popular with the locals. If you're in the mood for a flirt fest, your best bet is to arrive early, order a glass of Muller-Thurgau and make new friends while you wait. Dinner $50-$70.

The Tipping Points

The rules of tipping in New York are fairly straightforward.

- Server: 15-20 percent, depending on the service.

- Bartender: $1-2/drink, depending on your largesse.

- Coat check: $2/coat.

- Restroom attendant: $1-$2 depending on how many grooming products or breath mints you decide to pilfer from the stash.

While you can exceed the above guidelines, tipping less is frowned upon. Also, tipping the maitre d' is not customary in New York.

Note

Check out the New York Nibbles section of the Get in the Mood chapter for the best local food markets, gourmet goodies, and street eats.

DANCING DIVAS

> "If nightclubs aren't your thing,
>   that doesn't mean you have to forgo dancing."

Dancing in New York City is more than a nighttime activity – it's an event. For most New Yorkers, heading out to a club is usually the finale to an evening of cavorting, after dinner and drinks at a different location. Whether you're looking for a place to go with the girls or hoping to meet a mover and a shaker, you'll find what you're looking for here. NYC offers every imaginable type of music to shake your booty to, and if you're lucky, you just might find a terrific partner while you're at it, too!

Learn the Moves

These days, taking a dance class is not just a novelty activity for an evening's entertainment. Sexy city gals are regularly shimmying and shaking their way to a fun time at some of the hottest classes around. The instructors are ready and you don't need a partner to get started. The following places are not only fun for learning new steps – you can also meet the most interesting people when you open yourself up to new experiences!

SALSA SALSA DANCE STUDIO

55 FOURTH AVENUE
718 602 1322
BROOKLYN, PACIFIC ST STATION
WWW.SALSASALSADANCESTUDIO.COM

Bring your friends or sign up for a class by yourself at this brightly lit and easy-to-find dance studio that focuses on salsa. Friendly instructors teach the "on the 2" Mambo style, including turn patterns and shines. The low rates make it worth the trek out to Brooklyn.

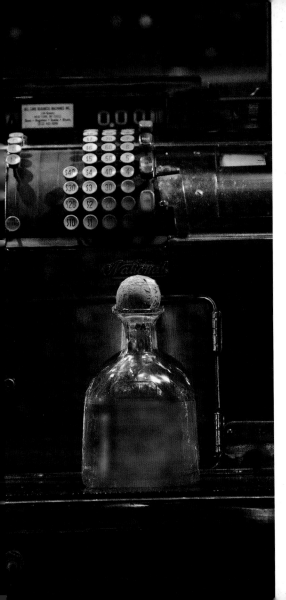

STEPPING OUT STUDIOS
37 W 26TH STREET 9TH FL
646 742 9400
FLATIRON DISTRICT, 28TH ST STATION
WWW.STEPPINGOUTSTUDIOS.COM

Fun group classes for beginners who want to dance without taking things too seriously. Add a waltz and a foxtrot to your repertoire, then join the monthly All Night Milonga held in a grand ballroom.

DANCE STUDIO 101
101 LAFAYETTE STREET, 2ND FL
212 431 7134
CHINATOWN, CANAL ST STATION
WWW.DANCESTUDIO101.COM

Olga's International Latin Group Class will help you add to your basic skills while a monthly Argentine Tango night gives students a chance to strut their stuff.

BROADWAY DANCE CENTER
322 W 45TH STREET, 3RD FL
212 582 9304
THEATER DISTRICT, 42ND ST STATION
WWW.BROADWAYDANCECENTER.COM

The instructors will encourage you give it your all in one of their fun hip-hop classes. The bright, clean studio space makes this location an ideal one.

Stepping Out

The days of Studio 54 may be over, but New York City still offers the best in nightlife, whether you're an expert or just enthusiastic dancer. Don't worry about feeling out of place – although twenty-somethings do dominate some of the venues, all of the clubs listed here are places where you'll find a satisfyingly adult clientele (frat boys in baseball caps and t-shirts need not apply). When you're feeling ready to try your moves out in a club, throw caution to the wind and head out to one or more of these fun venues!

LQ

511 LEXINGTON AVENUE
212 593 7575
MIDTOWN EAST, GRAND CENTRAL STATION
WWW.LQNY.COM

Wednesday night is Legends of Salsa night at this boisterous club, and there are plenty of male leads, dressed
with Cuban flair, to choose from. Leave the jeans and
other casual pieces at home – dressing up will give you
a better chance of getting in the door. Expect to pay a
cover charge. If you can find your way onto the list, you
won't have to wait outside.

PACHA

618 W 46TH STREET
212 209 7500
HELL'S KITCHEN, 42ND ST STATION
WWW.PACHANYC.COM

This amazingly decadent club was first born in Ibiza, and
the NYC venue lives up to the hype. With house and
hip-hop music, a maze of staircases leading to different
dance floors and a royal décor with mosaics and mirrors,
Pacha is definitely an "it" spot. The beautifully dressed
clientele compete for attention with go-go shower dancers who get all wet as they bust a move.

PINK ELEPHANT CLUB

527 27TH STREET
212 463 0000
CHELSEA, 23RD ST STATION
WWW.PINKELEPHANTCLUB.COM

The gorgeous décor evoking St. Tropez makes up for the
relatively small dance floor at this Chelsea hot spot. If
you don't mind being pressed up against a good-looking
stranger, there's lots of fun to be had. Groove the night
away to house or trance music as you mingle amongst
the Euro-crowd. Getting through the door can be tricky
but it's worth being appraised to party here.

KUSH

191 CHRYSTIE STREET
212 677 7328
LOWER EAST SIDE, 2ND AVENUE STATION
WWW.THEKUSHNYC.COM

A Moroccan décor featuring warm lights, flickering
candles and organic Hookahs sets the scene for some
of the most fun dancing to be had in the city. Spinning
everything from 80s music to today's pop hits, Kush's
DJs play to the crowd, are open to requests and know
how to fill the dance floor. Young professionals dominate the scene.

S.O.B.'S
204 VARICK
212 243 4940
SOHO, HOUSTON ST STATION
WWW.SOBS.COM

The club features Latin and Samba but the real draw is Basement Bhangra, where you can move your body to Bollywood beats. The club attracts an interesting crowd and everyone is here to have a good time. The cover charge fluctuates – look for frequent $5 specials. If you're into mixing with a more mature crowd, this is the perfect spot for a dance lesson or simply a night out on the town.

GRIFFIN
50 GANSEVOORT ST
212 255 6676
MEATPACKING DISTRICT, 14TH ST STATION
WWW.THEGRIFFINNY.COM

Dance among the beautiful people at this hidden hot-spot. The chandeliers and velvet banquettes decorate this space frequented celebrities and everyday New Yorkers alike. Located in the Meatpacking District, the party doesn't get going until late night. A mix of house, hip-hop and Top 40 keeps everyone happy. And if you get up on one of the couches and lose control…so be it!

MARQUEE
289 10TH AVE
646 473 0202
CHELSEA, 23RD ST STATION
MARQUEENY.COM

If you're lucky, the bouncer might let you skip the line and the cover charge and head right onto the dance floor where you'll move your body for hours to hip-hop beats. If you're looking to have an intimate gathering, this isn't the place! The crowd here tends to dress in expensive, barely-there clothing, and unlike most clubs there's a good male-to-female ratio of patrons.

SWING 46
349 W 46TH ST
212 262 9554
THEATER DISTRICT, 42ND ST STATION
WWW.SWING46.COM

If you're the type of gal who wears dresses, red lipstick and has a penchant for all things 1940s, then you've found your home at Swing 46. Don't be afraid to don your sexiest Dita Von Teese getup – you won't be the only one at this old fashioned supper club with live jazz and swing bands. Take a lesson, then go for a spin on the dance floor or order up a Scotch and admire the pros as they cut up the dance floor.

Note

Many of the bars in the Art of Drinking section of this chapter also turn into dance venues later in the evening.

Return of the Mega-Clubs

In the 1990s, long before the lounge movement brought us civilized conversation over cocktails, clubbing was about massive venues packed to the rafters with bodies ecstatically dancing to the thumping music. Well hold onto your ear plugs, because they're back. As we go to press, two mega-clubs are getting ready to open their doors in Manhattan. **District 36** (www.D36NYC.com) and the Manchester-based legend **Sankeys** (www.sankeysnyc.com) are both large enough to hold at least 1000 clubbers and equipped with the latest sound system technology to attract the top DJ talent from around the world.

Naughty Note

If nightclubs aren't you thing, that doesn't mean you have to forgo dancing. Many Manhattan bars have great music and New Yorkers are not shy about moving a few bar stools out of the way to create their own little dance floor. If the music moves you, just go with it!

Where's the Party?

If you're searching for the hottest dance parties on any given night or the latest in nightlife news, use the following resources to find out who's DJing, who's playing live music and whether it's worth the trip! You're sure to end up with plenty of places to put on your dance card.

- **ClubPlanet.com** This website features the best bars, lounges and clubs in NYC, with pics from last night's hottest parties. Their witty articles will help you navigate the club scene like a pro.

- **City Search** At newyork.citysearch.com venues are broken down by category (ie; DJ, live music, late night scene). You'll find insider reviews by experts and real New Yorkers on what's hot – and not!

- *Time Out New York* Pick up the print edition of TONY or go to newyork.timeout.com for critics' club picks for each day of the week, the best dance clubs, and the best parties on the scene.

- *New York* **magazine** Need a place to tango, a dance club with great martinis or an all-night dance party? New York Mag comes out with a yearly "best of" list at www.nymag.com/bestofny/nightlife.

Dressed to the Nines

Wondering what's appropriate attire for your night out at a club? Obviously you want to wear something that will make the doorman pull aside the velvet rope. But the key to looking like a sexy New Yorker is to not go too overboard on jewelry, makeup and other accessories. NYC club-goers definitely rock the trends, but they don't wear all of them at once. Showing up in too-skimpy clothes will make you look like you're trying too hard – or worse, peg you as "Bridge and Tunnel" (ie: a suburbanite who comes to the city to party on the weekends). A good rule to follow: showcase one feature at a time, whether it's a cleavage-baring top, or smoky eyes. When in doubt, stick with black pants, pretty skirts and flirty dresses. But don't be afraid to risk a statement piece. New York women like to be on the cutting edge!

Sexy Shows

> *"Some of the biggest fans of the burlesque revival are women."*

New York is known worldwide for its shows, but ladies in search of something with a bit more kick – or kink – will find it quite a few steps off Broadway. From sassy to shocking, engaging to erotic, here are a few of the city's sexiest shows…

The Burlesque Revival

Think burlesque is nothing more than a glamorized strip show? Then you've been missing out on some fabulously frisky entertainment. Forget about images of silicon-injected bimbos gyrating lewdly in front of a male audience. Forget about naked bodies straddling stripper poles and g-strings stuffed with dollar bills. With its focus on theatrical performance and gorgeous packaging, burlesque is both fun and witty, with far more sex appeal than a mere strip show could ever hope to possess.

Burlesque began during the years of vaudeville in the 1840s with women coming on stage to perform bawdy comedic or musical skits in revealing costumes while the main performers changed sets and costumes. Naturally, this became the most popular part of the show and burlesque was born. In the early years their performances often poked fun at bourgeois society and questioned the "proper" place of women in the Victorian era. In the late 1860s, Lydia Thompson's British burlesque troupe became New York's biggest theatrical sensation with their hit show *Ixion* (1868), a mythological spoof with women in revealing tights playing men's roles. In later years burlesque acquired a more glamorous reputation with pinup stars like Lili St Cyr, Gypsy Rose Lee and Ann Corio.

"Anything worth doing is worth doing slowly."
GYPSY ROSE LEE, BURLESQUE DANCER

By the 1920s, the flesh-revealing aspects of burlesque started to eclipse the theatrical element, with regular police raids on venues that dared to bare all. By 1937 New York State authorities passed laws banning these risqué shows, and the burlesque scene slowly disappeared. The new popularity of Hollywood and Broadway shows gave the masses another outlet for entertainment, while the growth of the porn industry in the 1950s delivered to male audiences the "happy ending" that burlesque could only suggest.
Of course it's no surprise that women themselves were responsible for bringing back the glamorous art of burlesque in the early 1990s. Today New York City is the pulsing heart of a thriving neo-burlesque scene

that is slowly spreading around the globe to Paris, London and Berlin. "The Burlesque revival took place in New York because the scene was ripe for it," says Slipper Room owner and vaudeville performer James Habacker. "The scene is the child of Andy Warhol's factory and Charles Ludlam's Ridiculous Theatrical Company. It started as a lark around fifteen years ago; a bunch of us who had come up in the East Village were bored with the whole dance music scene and wanted to bring some fun back into nightlife."

Introducing Neo-Burlesque

The biggest difference between burlesque striptease and mere stripping is that for 99% of the show, the women are artfully covered by feathers, fans, bath bubbles, balloons or other creative props. The art of the tease lies in not revealing anything until the very end. Even then, pasties (with spinning tassels, of course) and g-strings mean performers are never completely in the buff. Each dancer chooses a colorful persona that goes far beyond just a stage name, with themed costumes and performance styles that can be seriously sexy, sweetly charming, or side-splitting hilarious.

While there are some performers who still focus on performing classic burlesque in fans and feathers, Neo-Burlesque (aka New Burlesque) has taken Manhattan by storm. This is an urban, edgier version of the familiar striptease, where anything goes in terms of style, from dramatic and slow burn to feminist and queer. Even the gentlemen get in on the act with their own "boylesque" shows to challenge sexual as well as social norms.

Naughty Note

Learn the moves yourself with classes at Jo Whedon's NY School of Burlesque, more info in the Erotic Education section of the Get in the Mood chapter.

Some of the biggest fans of the burlesque revival are women. And what's there not to love? It's sexy, sardonic, witty and often inspiring. Harking back to its anti-conformist origins, the neo-burlesque scene embraces women of all shapes and sizes, from the Rubenesque to the Amazonian. It shows how women hold the reigns of their own sexual prowess, becoming powerful goddesses of their own making rather than simply the objects of someone else's fantasy. And, of course, there are the costumes. From feathers, fishnets and fake eyelashes to satin, sparkles, and six-inch stilettos, it's the dream wardrobe of every woman's inner femme fatale.

And while you'll still find shows that could cause even the worldliest women to blush, burlesque is no longer just a part of the underground counter-culture. Thank (or blame) Hollywood and Madison Avenue for the mainstream popularity of this once maligned performance art, as burlesque superstar Dita von Teese appears in upscale cosmetic and liquor advertisements, and singing divas Cher and Christina Aguilera headlined the 2010 film *Burlesque*.

Where to Get Your Fix

The burlesque scene in the city is filled with such a variety, it promises to be a pleasurable experience over and over again. Manhattan boasts some of the top internationally known burlesque stars including the World Famous "Bob", Dirty Martini, Amber Ray, the Potani Sisters, and Veronica Varlow. Fans can usually find a burlesque event on any given night, from the famous Slipper Room shows to Coney Island's summertime "Burlesque on the Beach".

"Burlesque has a history of flourishing in New York," says Jo Whedon, Headmistress and founder of the New York School of Burlesque. "There were famous topless shows in Paris, and burlesque came to NYC in 1868 in the form of Lydia Thompson and her British Blondes, but burlesque striptease evolved right here in New York as a unique American phenomenon. Performers have had lots of time and a big community to support it, and to keep the School of Burlesque busy!"

"It doesn't matter what size or shape you are. Burlesque is about feeling positive about who you are, about knowing how to shake what you have and being proud of it."

BABY DOE, BURLESQUE DANCER

The Lower East Side currently holds court over Gotham's burlesque scene, though shows are starting to make their way uptown as dancers continue to find creative ways to turn any venue, no matter how small, into a burlesque stage. Going to a show with girlfriends is great because you can talk about which new moves you are going steal to incorporate into your repertoire. Going to a burlesque show on a date whether with a partner or a potential partner is perfect for the art of seduction, especially when it is your brilliant idea. It shows that you are confident in your own skin, while showing off your naughty side of being a voyeur. The audiences tend to dress casual, fitting with the location of the artsy funky scene downtown, but no one will fault you for dressing up, if you dare.

SLIPPER ROOM

167 ORCHARD STREET
LOWER EAST SIDE, SECOND AVENUE STATION
TEL 212 253 7426
WWW.SLIPPERROOM.COM

Some of the biggest stars in the industry have twirled their tassels on the hallowed stage of the Slipper Room, known as the city's "True Home of Burlesque" since 1999. While some acts have been running since the opening, there's always something new in the eclectic program of neo-burlesque and vaudeville shows presented by a talented host. Be sure to pack your sense of adventure: the risqué freak show atmosphere often pushes the limits of taste in typical New York in-your-face style. "I've never put any limits on the level of experimentation that people were allowed to explore," says founder James Habacker. "What is known as the New York style of burlesque, satirical comedy, strip tease, and variety acts; performance art that entertains and challenges, is really the Slipper Room style of burlesque." In 2010 the Slipper Room closed to begin expansion renovations, opening the top floor for extra high ceilings to accommodate aerial acts and acrobatics. Until they reopen in late 2011, look for their Slipper Room in Exile parties on their website. Entry $5.

SHAKEN AND STIRRED

THE DELANCEY: 168 DELANCEY STREET
LOWER EAST SIDE, DELANCEY-ESSEX STREET STATION
TEL 212 254 9920
WWW.SUGARSHACKBURLESQUE.COM

Sugar Shack Burlesque hosts Manhattan's popular burlesque dance party, Shaken and Stirred, featuring the city's most beloved burlesque stars, free shots and some of the hottest go-go dancers in town. Getting you onto the dance floor is DJ Jess and your hostess for the evening, Miss "RunAround" Sue, who encourages audience participation in the infamous Go-Go Contest and – for those in a truly naughty mood – the Makeout Minute. It can and does get scandalous, because by this time everyone is tipsy from the vodka shots and will do almost anything to get on stage to make out with the sexy host. And even if you're not up for this public display of affection yourself, it's certainly the best part of the show. Wednesdays at 9pm, no cover.

KITTY NIGHTS

AT THE BAR ON A: 170 AVE A AT 11TH STREET
EAST VILLAGE, 1ST AVENUE STATION
TEL 212 353 8231
WWW.KITTYNIGHTS.COM

Now a staple in the downtown burlesque scene with a mix of international and veteran dancers, Kitty Nights is known as the best venue for seeing new and upcoming dancing sex kittens. Shows are every Sunday night at 9pm, with a unique and diverse lineup of beautiful performers of all ages, races, shapes and sizes. The show changes each week, with regular surprise guest appearances. For just $5, expect a night filled with kittens, tassels, pasties, glitter, and the colorful locals of the Lower East Side. Meow!

NURSE BETTIE

106 NORFOLK STREET
LOWER EAST SIDE, DELANCEY-ESSEX STREET STATION
TEL 212 477 7515
WWW.NURSEBETTIELES.COM

If you're looking for an excuse to press up against your date (or a handsome stranger), this kitsch and cozy pinup bar with the large Bettie Page inspired posters packs them in so tightly you're bound to make some sexy new friends by the end of the night. Making the bump and grind complete is the sassy show, where burlesque babes such as Calamity Chang have been known to spank a willing audience member or two. If you'd rather avoid bending over, volunteer instead for one of the show's sexy games. This classy joint offers insanely priced cocktails with clever names like Au Pear. Follow them on Twitter (@nursebettienyc) for the nightly password for a free drink. Thursdays or Fridays at 9:30pm, no cover.

Naughty tip

Always get to the shows early to secure seats; reservations are not possible, and standing for hours in stiletto heels is just not sexy.

THE BOX

189 CHRYSTIE STREET
LOWER EAST SIDE, BOWERY STATION
TEL 917 280 5977
WWW.THEBOXNYC.COM

The burlesque acts aren't the only thing people find out-rageous at this exclusive venue on the Lower East Side. So take up your Manhattan friends' offer to treat you to a night on the town, sweetly ask them to book a table, and be prepared for a raucous party with the flamboyant clientele and over-the-top performers. Open Tues-Sat from 11pm; shows start after 1am.

"I advocate glamour. Every day. Every minute."
—DITA VON TEESE, BURLESQUE DANCER

Burlesque Events

Get your burlesque fix at the annual **New York Burlesque Festival**, featuring the best per-formers from around the world, from the sexy starlets to the feisty newcomers. The fun takes place every Fall in some of the city's hottest clubs and lounges with an enthusiastic audience of fans from far and wide. www.thenewyork-burlesquefestival.com

When the city heats up it's time to head out to Coney Island for the popular **Burlesque on the Beach**, a revival of old style burlesque with sideshow freaks, strange women, new vaude-ville and live music. Thursday and Friday nights from May through September. www.coneyis-land.com

Find out about more burlesque events around town in local papers such as the **Village Voice** and **Time Out**, or **Brooklyn Ed's Burlesque Calendar:** www.edbarnas.com.

Eye Candy for the Ladies

While we ladies always appreciate the seductive art of burlesque, sometimes we just want to leave all decorum behind for a bit of PDA -- public display of abs. Men's abs, that is. There are few places where women can blatantly ogle, scream and applaud at the sight of finely chiseled male bodies, so forget about ladylike restraint and get ready to let your hair down with your closest friends for a night of masculine bravado and bulging muscles.

Naughty Tip

Want to avoid any embarrassing photographic evidence of your evening out with the ladies? Come prepared with carnival masks or even fun party wigs to keep your identity under wraps.

What to Expect

Swallow your cool dignity and join the gaggles of giggling women who have come to Manhattan to give their bachelorette or birthday girl the time of her life. The general format is the same for each club: shows are every Friday and Saturday, with the door open at 8pm and the show 9pm-11pm. After being seated by the hunky bartenders, you'll be served shots and music will be played for dancing. The show has the usual repertoire of sailor, doctor, policeman costumes, lip-synching and acrobatics while an MC encourages the audience to scream and cheer. NY State laws prohibit the Full Monty, so anything – but not everything – goes as the dancers strip down to their bulging g-strings. The VIP ladies of the evening (who paid extra for the "hot seat") are hoisted up to the stage and into the arms of the well-oiled dancers as enthusiastic participants in the show, with the goal seemingly to get them into as many compromising positions as possible for the amusement of their friends. Be sure to wear trousers or fun panties you don't mind flashing in case you're in a skirt or dress. After the show is done, the dancers leave and the club opens to the public so the party can continue on the dance floor until the wee hours. The coat check, drinks and lap dances can quickly add up, so bring plenty of cash (including singles for the dancers), and make sure you have enough for the taxi ride home.

Hunk Mania

M2 LOUNGE, 530 WEST 28TH STREET
CHELSEA, 34TH STREET STATION
TEL 917 470 9829
WWW.HUNKMANIA.COM

No lady is left behind at Hunk mania, where the attentive lap dancers and table service bartenders flirt with the women in the audience while the main show is taking place on the stage. and if a particularly impressive set of abs come your way, know that touching is not only allowed, it's encouraged, especially if you splurge on a lap dance. And you won't even have to wait in line when the glitzy M2 Lounge club opens to the public after the show. the show costs $25, $45 for ViP status.

Savage Men

TEL 888 572 8243
WWW.SAVAGEMEN.COM

The Savage Men shows take place in different venues around Midtown, often with conference-style seating of chairs in rows. There is less interaction between the dancers and the audience aside from the VIPs, although lap dances and massages are available for an additional fee. Entry $20, $40 for VIP status.

Manhattan Men

191 ESSEX STREET
LOWER EAST SIDE, 2ND AVENUE STATION
TEL 347 852 0157
WWW.MANHATTANMEN.COM

Ladies on the shy side will appreciate the "no photos" rule at Manhattan Men, known more for its choreographed dancing than raunchy gyrating. Of course, it's still a male strip show, so expect an off-off-off Broadway revue to ADD pop music. Folding tables and chairs are set up for each group with private dances taking place in the lounge. entry is $20 on Friday, $25 on Saturday, and $45 for ViP status.

NAUGHTY ADVENTURES

Swinging New York

Fasten your garter belt, ladies. We're not in Kansas anymore. Consider everything you've read up to this chapter to be merely a warm-up, a sort of erotic preparation to get you in the mood for the juiciest bite of the Big Apple.

Because now it's time for Truth or Dare: How far are you willing to go? Whether you're simply dying of curiosity about what really happens behind closed doors or looking to dive right into the naughty side of the city, we give you the insider scoop on getting a piece of the action. And make no mistake about it: New York City is all about action. This chapter will provide you with not only the best of the naughty addresses, but also a thorough briefing on what to expect, how to behave properly, and plenty of tips on etiquette, wardrobe, and finding the perfect venue for a decadent night of debauchery on the town.

The Concept

Swinger's clubs, also referred to as sex clubs or sex parties, are places where consenting adults go to meet, mingle…and more if there's chemistry. And yes, "more" means sex, ladies. Known commonly as "wife-swapping" in the 1970s, these clubs became popular with married suburbanites looking to inject a bit of excitement into their sex lives. Today anything goes, with sexually liberated singles, couples, and even triples coming together for mutual fun and pleasure.

"Home is heaven and orgies are vile, But you need an orgy, once in a while."
—FREDERIC OGDEN NASH

What to Expect

At this point you might be imagining sordid orgies where you're expected to check your clothes at the door and surrender yourself to a crowd of sex-crazed strangers. Relax. The reality is a touch more sophisticated in most cases. Not all clubs require you to disrobe, and the ones that do still allow for towels or lingerie. Like many nightclubs, there's usually a bar, a dance floor, sometimes a buffet where couples can strike up casual conversations. Mia Martina, aka "Mia on Top", the woman behind the popular podcast "I Want Your Sex" on the NY sex party scene, says there are many misconceptions about what's expected at these parties. "Don't worry that if you want to go to a sex party, you are signing up for having a huge orgy or seeing your partner have sex with others. Or if you go to a bondage party you will be gagged and suspended upside down. The sex scene is very beginner friendly and you are never pressured to do anything you are uncomfortable with. One can attend a sex party or a kink event and not participate. No one will think less of you."

Swinger's clubs are just like regular clubs except that you get to dress sexier and be more daring in a setting that gives you the freedom to do what you couldn't do in other clubs. It's a safe environment where sexual activity is encouraged, but never required. What's fun is that you have the choice. Even if nothing happens, it's exciting just knowing that sex is a possibility. A very real possibility, which fosters an erotically-charged atmosphere of lingering glances, suggestive smiles and overt seduction as couples size up potential playmates.

Of course, you shouldn't expect the average sex party to look like the orgy scene out of *Eyes Wide Shut* either. Not everyone at an event is going to be thin, beautiful, and have impeccable manners. Mia warns ladies to be prepared for the creepy guy factor: "This is a guy who may stare obsessively at women, masturbate in a corner for the party's duration, or touch others without invitation. Party hosts do what they can to limit the creepy guy factor by having a screening process to attend events, by having couples-only events and by securing couples-only spaces within the venue."

Women of a Certain Age

While the majority of women at these parties are in the 25-45 age group, sexy women (and men) of all ages are welcome. Style counts, so dress to impress and don't forget that there's nothing sexier than self-confidence.

Getting Friendly

And how to make it clear if you are interested in frolicking with fellow swingers? At the bar or dance floor this is similar to any other club, by striking up conversation or dancing a bit closer. After a few cocktails and a bit of dirty dancing, most of the couples – sometimes alone, sometimes with another couple – disappear into the back rooms or anywhere there are mattresses arranged specifically for play. Rooms might be small and dark for just one couple or large and mirrored for many couples to cavort side by side on large beds or mattresses. Sometimes there are rooms with locking doors and one-way mirrors or windows so that couples can engage in some very public displays of affection without the risk of anyone else asking to join in. Other rooms might even have a light bondage theme where you can tie up or lock your partner. There are often as many voyeurs as there are exhibitionists, watching others before they decide whether to participate or not.

Proper Etiquette

A soft caress on the arm (or the closest body part) is what usually constitutes a pass. You can caress back, or politely shake your head no. Some couples just go to have fun with each other, not to mix with others. In either case, it's important to respectfully communicate your boundaries. Don't be afraid to use body language. Be subtle when making a pass of your own, and never insist. The secret to having a positive experience in any club is a relaxed attitude and a sense of humor. Stay open-minded, have fun, and don't get too offended by the inevitable invitations…or rebuffs.

Along with groping without permission, drinks are forbidden in the back rooms to keep spillage on mattresses to a minimum. If at any time you get uncomfortable in the back rooms, you can always excuse yourself and go back to the public areas or find the host. On couples-only nights, men are typically not allowed to venture into the back rooms without their partners. If you're unsure about the correct protocol, don't be afraid to ask another couple. Your neophyte status is the perfect ice-breaker.

Your First Time
The best approach is to go with an open mind and keep your expectations in check. Like any nightclub, the atmosphere will depend on the crowd on any given night. Go on "couples only" evenings if you want to avoid an overbalance of men to women, and get there early before it gets crowded so you can slowly acclimate to the setting. The back room action doesn't usually begin right away, so you can relax first at the bar or buffet if there is one. When in a couple, have your ground rules established in advance, not in the heat of the moment. Then just see where the mood takes you. Remember, you're never obliged to join in.

Health & Safety
Despite the sinfully decadent activities going on in the back rooms, the clientele of swinger's clubs are generally more polite and well-behaved than in regular nightclubs. After all, a club's reputation is largely dependent on the comfort of its female clientele. "The staff tends to look after the attendees, especially the single women," says Mia. Anyone displaying rude or pushy behavior will be escorted immediately to the door, so make sure you signal any bad apples to your host. "You are not being a tattle-tale if you do this," Mia insists. "The host wants everyone to feel comfortable, especially single women." And if one night of fun is all you're looking for, at least in a swinger's club you never have to decide "his place or mine" or find yourself alone with a stranger. For health and hygiene, Mia recommends packing a small purse with condoms, lubrication, hand sanitizer, and a pack of tissues. Although many events provide these items, they may run out, may not be the kind you like, or may not be so readily available when you need them.

A Bit of Advice

A glass (or two) of Champagne may help you relax, but don't drink so much that your judgment will be affected. There's nothing ladylike about drunken debauchery, even in a swinger's club.

What about Unaccompanied Women?

In the swinger scene, single women are known as unicorns for their rarity. It's a couple's scene, but many are looking to have a threesome with another woman, so single women are in high demand.

"I have been to parties where I am the only single person in a crowd of 40 couples," says Mia. "It has been either feast or famine with many couples vying for my attention or not talking to me at all. The thing to remember is that as nervous as you are to be out in a couple's scene by yourself, the couples are more nervous than you. Remember you are the unicorn and you ultimately have the upper hand and can write your ticket for the night." If you find that no one is approaching you, don't be afraid to make the first move yourself.

Sex, Spirits & the State

While New York City may be known for its naughty nightlife, local laws make it illegal to mix full nudity with the sale of alcohol. The sex party scene works around this by introducing the concepts of "On-Premise", "Off-Premise" and "BYOB". Parties designated as "Off-Premise" take place in bars, clubs, and private lofts where alcohol is sold, so no sex is allowed and participants have to make sure their most intimate body parts are covered (pasties and g-strings usually do the trick). "On-Premise" parties take place in private venues where the only alcohol that is served is brought by the participants ("BYOB"). Simply check in your bottle with the bartender, who will put a label on it with your name. The venue provides ice and mixers (generally tonic, soda, Coke). Even though it's your own, don't forget to tip the bartenders for the service.

Sex Parties & Clubs

There are few actual sex clubs in New York, as many organizers prefer to keep things fresh, exclusive and neatly outside strict state regulations by hosting private parties in different venues. We've selected the best on the scene for you ladies, particularly those suited for newcomers and frequented by a discerning clientele.

ONE LEG UP
PRIVATE PARTIES
ON-PREMISE "EAT IN" PARTIES (BYOB)
OFF-PREMISE "TAKE OUT" PARTIES
WWW.ONELEGUPNYC.COM

If you have time for only one erotic escapade while visiting Manhattan, choose the crème de la crème of sex parties to indulge your fantasies. For over 12 years, the New Yorker known enigmatically as Palagia has been hosting sensual gatherings with a flair for the theatrical. Her bacchanalian costume parties have themes like Seven Deadly Sins and Dangerous Liaisons, featuring burlesque performers, go-go dancers, acrobats, or percussionists. Whet your appetite at a "Take Out" event, where couples and single ladies decked out in that night's risqué dress code meet in bars and lounges for fun and naughty fondling. To graduate to the taboo-free "Eat In" parties where anything and everything goes (including clothing when the 12:30am "Undies-only" bell rings), you'll have to pass a strict screening process. This keeps out the creeps and ensures a safe atmosphere where like-minded swingers can relax and play. It doesn't hurt to be young, rich and beautiful to join this Country Club of Sex, but as they say, personality goes a long way.

Practical Info
"Take Out" Parties are $75 for couples, $15 for single ladies. Open to the public; in bars and clubs; sex not permitted. "Eat in" Parties are $250 for couples, $50 for single ladies. Membership required ($199 quarterly dues); in private venues; sex permitted. Members also get discounted entry to "take Out" Parties.

A Bit of Advice

It's not uncommon at sex parties and clubs to find yourself shedding articles of clothing from one room to another. Either avoid wearing your most expensive French lace bra, or be sure to keep a close eye on your precious belongings lest you find they've been "cleaned up" and thrown away towards closing time.

SKIN

PRIVATE PARTY
OFF-PREMISE
WWW.SKINPARTY.COM

Perhaps you don't think of yourself as a swinger, but you'd still like to go out dancing somewhere sexy where you can show a little skin…or a lot. These parties held in large NY clubs are all about pleasing the ladies. Single men are never admitted and sex on the premises is not allowed, so expect a wild sorority party atmosphere without the backroom hanky panky. less exclusive than the One leg Up parties, the crowd at Skin tends to attract a younger (25-40 years old) clientele from the tri-State area who come into Manhattan for a naughty weekend getaway. Women rule the roost here and get to choose their dance partners, often teasing the vastly outnumbered men by dancing with each other. the gentlemen don't seem to mind enjoying the Sappho-erotic show from the sidelines.

Practical Info

Entry at the door is free for ladies, $100 for couples. Cash only, credit cards not accepted. Be sure to dress sexy (gentlemen should avoid sneakers and jeans) and show some skin! If you become a member, entrance is free for the ladies and $80 for couples with advance ticket purchase. To become a member submit an essay and photos to www.virtualviplounge.com.

SCHOOL OF SEX "BEHIND CLOSED DOORS"

PRIVATE PARTY
ON-PREMISE
WWW.SCHOOLOFSEX.NET

For ladies looking for a little bit more hand-holding before diving into the world of swingers clubs and sex parties, the School of Sex begins each of its "Behind Closed Doors" parties with an orientation session for newcomers. "Swing School" is run by a real couple in their 20s, Jasmine and David, aka Sex Kitten & Rocco, who share their own experiences and offer tips on how to enjoy the party. Afterward couples and single ladies (no single men are admitted) mingle and share their own experiences and advice. The more experienced swingers join the party later in the evening when things start to heat up. a masseur gets the ladies in the mood while drinks are served by topless bartenders and couples go behind curtained-off areas to romp on beds and mattresses. Some parties have belly dancing lessons, Kama Sutra demonstrations, or the "Sybian" orgasm machine to spice things up. Membership is required to attend Behind Closed Doors (photos and an essay). Whether you're a newcomer, exhibitionist, voyeur or serious swinger, you'll fit right in if you're an attractive woman or couple aged 21-40, as Jasmine and David claim to have the hottest (and youngest) members in town. The parties take place in a large Manhattan loft space with outdoor terrace. Ladies can also attend informal social hour events called Girls Uncorked every third Thursday for wine and conversation, no membership required.

Practical Info
Entry to Behind Closed Doors $140 for couples, $50 for ladies, including drinks and snacks. Membership dues are $30 quarterly. Girls Uncorked events are free with registration online, each guest is asked to bring a bottle of wine.

Beyond Voyeurism

The best clubs and parties don't allow men to go into the back rooms or curtained off areas without their partners. While watching and being watched is all part of the fun, this eliminates the gawking herds of men found in the less vigilant venues.

CHEMISTRY
PRIVATE PARTY
ON-PREMISE (BYOB)
WWW.CHEMISTRY-NYC.COM

Looking for a more alternative vibe to the Manhattan scene? Chemistry's inclusive parties, usually held in a Brooklyn loft, attract an artsy clientele with a wide range in age, personal style and sexual preference. The hosts SheilaMonster and KennyBlunt focus on creating a pressure-free, lively party scene with live DJs, a large dance floor, and regular themed parties, while guests come dressed in everything from fetish or bondage gear to lingerie, cocktail dresses or casual clothing. Flame throwers, hula hoop dancers, and conversations about Tantric sex and naked yoga contribute to the overall "Burning Man" atmosphere guaranteed to set the stage for a wild and naughty night. For guests who are ready to take their dance floor moves to a horizontal position, there are curtained off areas equipped with futons and platform beds. Chemistry is for open-minded couples and ladies only, although some single males who have already come as part of a couple are invited when the number of single ladies is high.

Practical Info
Membership is $20 for couples, free for single ladies. Party entrance is $120 for couples and $12 "hold" for single ladies refunded after the party. Parties take place every 5-8 weeks.

LE TRAPEZE CLUB

17 EAST 27TH STREET
GRAMERCY PARK, 28TH ST. STATION
TEL 212 532 0298
WWW.LETRAPEZE.ORG
ON-PREMISE (BYOB)

Sex clubs in Manhattan tend to embrace the "seedy" reputation that the best parties work so hard to overcome, and
Le Trapeze is no different despite being the best-known
sex club in town. The lack of a membership requirement
makes it easier for out-of-town visitors to spontaneously
pop in for a frolic, but don't expect to be impressed by
the odd English pub décor. When you arrive, you and
your partner should check your belongings into a locker
and slip into a sexy nightie or lingerie ensemble (or wear
the provided towel). Stripping down to your underthings
is not a rule, but if you keep on your street clothes, you
may be the only one. Strappy flats are recommended for
ladies, since heels aren't allowed in the mattress rooms.
Newcomers are welcomed by Eli, the assistant manager
and DJ. After a tour of the dance floor, buffet and lounge,
head down "trapeze lane" to the naughty play rooms with
your partner – no singles allowed! If the doors are locked,
the couples inside prefer privacy. If they are unlocked it
means they're looking for others to join in. You can simply watch if that's your thing, although the dim red lighting and mattress-covered floors are probably best enjoyed
with your eyes wide shut.

Open Wednesday-Thursday 9pm-2am, $110 for couples. Friday-Saturday 9pm-4am, $120 for couples. Although it's labeled as "couples only" single females are admitted for $30. The clientele are very mixed in age, background and attractiveness. Wednesday nights are most popular with the serious swingers, with newcomers more present on the weekend. Communal showers are available, but the play areas are a bit on the sparse side for supplies, so be sure to bring your own hand wipes and protection.

Sex Club vs Private Parties

Discerning swingers in New York tend to favor the exclusive member-only parties rather than the often aesthetically-challenged sex clubs. Strict screening for the parties also helps cut down on the presence of paid female "escorts" which have been known to frequent the clubs where single men are allowed in. Since much of the enjoyment of swinging is about meeting like-minded couples and singles in a safe and comfortable setting, reputable sex party organizers don't allow this at their events.

Breaking the Ice

One of the best places to engage in conversation at sex parties is in line at the bar or restroom, since everyone tends to be there without their partner.

Recommended References for your Naughty Library

Hungry for more information on the world of swinging? Mia recommends these books, sure to get you into the swing of things!

• Swinging for Beginners: An Introduction to the Lifestyle by Kaye Bellemeade

• Opening Up: A Guide to Creating and Sustaining Open Relationships by Tristan Taormino

• The Lifestyle: A Look at the Erotic Rites of Swingers by Terry Gould

• The Ethical Slut: A Guide to Infinite Sexual Possibilities by Dossie Easton and Catherine A. Liszt

• Open: Love, Sex, and Life in an Open Marriage by Jenny Block

Fetish & Whips

Welcome to the dark side, ladies. Perhaps you only turned to this page out of curiosity, believing fetish just isn't your thing. But you may have already, dabbled in fetish or sadomasochistic dalliances. Doth thou protest, Madame? Consider, if you will, the seemingly innocent satin blindfold next to your bed, the fuzzy handcuffs you purchased with a wicked giggle, and the sexy corset and stockings you wore for his birthday. if you've ever allowed yourself to be tied to the bedposts or wore your three-inch stiletto heels while making love, then you're not quite the "fetish virgin" you think you are.

Once considered strictly deviant and underground, today fetish and SM imagery have infiltrated popular culture, from Lady Gaga's dominatrix-influenced outfits and the dominant/submissive role playing in The Secretary, to superheroes in skintight costumes and elaborate fantasy worlds of leather-clad warriors. And who doesn't love to vamp it up for Halloween? Safely disguised as our sexy alter egos, we become mysterious, intriguing, and audacious.

Playing these Bad Girl/Bad Boy roles can be a huge turn-on because, like in the movies or bodice-ripping novels, we know there isn't any real danger of getting hurt. Sexual tension builds during the drawn out power plays, inevitably leading to a pleasurable climax (pun intended) when the sparks start to fly. Intrigued? Curious? Whether daring or undecided, you don't need to be a convert to the fetish lifestyle in order to enjoy an exploratory dabble in the Manhattan scene, whose parties are more accessible and female-friendly than you might expect. You may find a whole new world of sexy fun awaiting your discovery. Or, in the least, a memorable travel tale. But first, a few essential pointers on etiquette, dress code, and what to expect as a naughty neophyte.

Naughtier Than You Think

According to the Kinsey Institute of Indiana University, 5-10% of Americans engage in light SM on at least an occasional basis. And if you've ever been blindfolded, tied up, or spanked by your lover during sex, you can count yourself among them.

Fetish vs BDSM? A Naughty Primer

BDSM is an umbrella acronym for activities that include Bondage/Discipline, Dominance/Submission, and Sadism/Masochism. There are subtle distinctions and overlapping between each practice, but in general BDSM is about psychological stimulation and physical sensations. It's an exchange of power based on trust with pleasure as the ultimate goal for both parties, even – despite appearances – when "pain" is involved. The important thing to keep in mind here is that it's nothing more than elaborate role play between consenting adults. As sex columnist Dan Savage says, BDSM role playing and power playing is like "cops and robbers for adults." Happily, for every man or woman who gets erotic pleasure out of tying up, whipping, and ordering someone else around, there's a soulmate out there who gets erotic pleasure out of being tied down, spanked, and obeying orders.

While BDSM concerns sexually arousing activities, fetishism is about sexually arousing objects such as high heels, seamed stockings, corsets, and clothing made from leather, rubber, latex, or PVC. Not all fetishists are into BDSM (and likewise, not all fetish parties have dungeons for BDSM activities), however there's a lot of overlap between the two communities since many BDSM practitioners use fetish objects and wear fetish clothing.

Sadomasochistic Literature

The term 'Sadism' comes from the French aristocrat Marquis de Sade (1740-1814), whose pornographic writings mirrored his own shockingly violent (and often non-consensual) sexual proclivities. His Austrian contemporary, the novelist Leopold von Sacher-Masoch (1836-1895), inspired the term 'Masochism' after romanticizing sexual servitude in his books such as Venus in Furs. One of the most scandalous sado-masochistic novels of the 20th century, The Story of O, was actually written by a woman, Pauline Réage, to impress her lover.

The Manhattan Scene

The S&M scene in Manhattan is primarily for those who practice the BDSM lifestyle. This is the realm of fantasy, where you get to dress up, meet other like-minded fetishists, and realize your wildest dreams – all within the bounds of consensual participation and respect for the other guests. While swinger's clubs are more about the unexpected and letting go for a night of fun, fetish parties are more like a stage for elaborate shows that are often planned in advance, complete with role-playing, costumes, and an appreciative audience. Bondage and whipping scenes take on the feel of performance art. But no matter how humble or flashy the event, these events are simply a way of bringing the underground into the open, where the thrill of being someone completely different in a very public setting adds to the excitement.

There are also very practical aspects to these venues. New Yorkers living in the city tend to have restricted living space and thin walls, hardly conducive to loud whipping sessions or bulky bondage equipment. Dungeons, whether in clubs or private parties, are safe places to play without worrying about calls from police responding to suspicious neighbors.

Sex in the BDSM Scene

Unlike the sex party scene, fetish parties and S&M clubs are strictly sex-free zones due to local laws… at least at public events. While the definition of what constitutes sex sometimes gets hazy à la Bill Clinton, a good guideline to follow is to avoid anything involving penetration or a "happy ending" unless you want to risk getting kicked off the playground. If your outfit and adventurous attitude captures attention at any of the BDSM events, you just might get an invitation to one of the private after-parties, where anything goes.

Who Goes?

Fetish parties bring together an incredibly diverse population of people of all ages, backgrounds, orientations and inclinations. You might encounter 20-something Goth clubbers covered in tattoos and piercings, a middle-aged dominatrix in a skin-tight rubber catsuit, a transvestite in a French maid outfit, or a masked woman being spanked by a distinguished gentleman dressed as a military officer.

Your First Time

If you're new to the scene, you might get the impression you're walking into a den of Hell's angels. But fear not, Ladies. As scary as a dungeon full of torture instruments looks, no one will simply grab you, tie you up and commence with a caning. The main purpose is to dress up and socialize with like-minded people, so newcomers shouldn't feel obliged to participate in any sadomasochistic activities typically reserved for experienced practitioners and their partners. Unlike swinger events, fetish/BSDM parties are open to couples, singles, or even groups of friends, as long as you're over 18 and properly dressed. "But this is not a zoo for gawking," explains one event organizer. "We welcome anyone genuinely interested in discovering the fetish/BDSM lifestyle."

What to Wear

Dress codes depend on the party, but you can't go wrong in any outfit made of leather, PVC or latex. Other options include sexy uniforms, Goth, Japanese manga, transvestite, and "bizarre" science fiction or fantasy looks. As a rule, the bigger the party, the more elaborate the outfits. Of course, you could simply get away with a "civilian" look of a leather skirt with sexy top and heels, all in black, but dressing up is part of the fun. Browse the racks of the city's excellent fetish clothing boutiques for inspiration (see Get in the Mood chapter).

Naughty Tip

If you don't arrive in your outfit, you can change inside and then leave your civilian clothes in the cloakroom. Space and privacy may be limited, so be savvy and wear something over your fetishwear that you can simply pull off when you arrive.

Fetish Etiquette

As in the swingers community, everyone is expected to observe the rule of mutual respect. An open mind and a sense of humor (without inappropriate giggling) can diffuse situations that might be potentially uncomfortable for newcomers. It's not uncommon for women to be approached by submissive men (usually on all fours) with specific requests such as: "May I worship your boots/shoes/feet?" or "Will you whip me?" If you're not keen on playing, a polite refusal will suffice. If you would like to watch the BDSM activities taking place in the "dungeon", remain as silent and discreet as possible. Voyeurs are welcome, but you should make an effort to avoid interrupting or interfering, just as you would in a theatre. And remember that no matter how disturbing, cruel or painful some acts may appear, these are simply very convincing performances between consenting adults living out their fantasies.

Safety

There's no harm in a bit of whipping and bondage between consenting adults, right? But do be aware that certain precautions need to be taken when playing these adult games. If you're new to the scene it's not a good idea to simply pick up a bullwhip and start cracking away at your partner's exposed flesh. Contrary to appearances, the goal isn't actually to cause any physical harm. You'll have no trouble finding an experienced hand at these clubs willing to demonstrate the proper technique — someone to show you the ropes, as they say. If you've already perfected your flogging form, then by all means feel free to inspect the eligible submissives at your disposal. Likewise, make sure you clearly communicate your own limits to any potential playmates if you find yourself on the receiving end of a naughty spanking.

"Whenever a taboo is broken, something good happens, something vitalizing. Taboos, after all, are only hangovers, the product of diseased minds, you might say, of fearsome people who hadn't the courage to live and who, under the guise or morality and religion, have imposed these things upon us."

—AMERICAN WRITER HENRY MILLER

S&M Parties

SUSPENSION

THE DELANCY, 168 DELANCY STREET
LOWER EAST SIDE, ESSEX OR DELANCY STATION
TEL 212 254 9920
SUSPENSIONNYC@GMAIL.COM

Three floors and a rooftop garden provide the perfect setting to bond (and get bound) with fellow fans of the BDSM scene, a diverse, younger crowd generally 25-40 years old. While there is dancing and couples cuddling in dark corners, most guests come to play out their bondage and corporal punishment fantasies. Dream of being suspended 12' in the air? They've got the equipment at Suspension. "Many experts in Japanese bondage come to this event to express themselves," says Kelley Dane, one of the party's hosts. At the party there are fetish ambassadors that will show newcomers around and make introductions. Those who make an effort to fit in with the hip, avantgarde vibe of Suspension are more likely to impress the doorman.

PRACTICAL INFO
Suspension parties take place the last Saturday of the month from 10pm. Entry is $30 if you're dressed in all black (no jeans or sneakers), or $15 if you're in fetish wear. More info at http://fetlife.com (search for NYC Fetish Tribe).

Every second Thursday of the month the Suspension organizers host Impact, a smaller sophisticated party with about 200 guests in an atmosphere that's more "kinky cocktails" than "dark dungeon." This party focuses on all kinds of impact play such as spanking, flogging and whipping. Same contact info, pricing and dress code as Suspension.

Noteworthy Fetish Events

One of the most extravagant fetish parties in New York with the cheeky name of "Smack" takes place twice a year, as a part of the Fetish Marathon in June and on Halloween, since 1996. This is the place where you should dress to the nines in your most fabulous fetish gear for drinking and schmoozing with the elite of the fetish/kink/BDSM scenes. The "Multimedia Play Party" includes performances, fashion shows, cutting edge music, video artists, a fully-equipped dungeon and dominatrix hosts.

smackfetish.com and
www.nyfetishmarathon.com

STIMULATE

CRASH MANSION, 199 BOWERY
LOWER EAST SIDE; BOWERY, SPRING OR 2ND AVE STATION
WWW.STIMULATE-ME.COM

Have you got the most fabulous fetish outfit to show off? This is your catwalk for every kind of look from Gothic Lolita and Steampunk to leather, corsetry and armor. The more striking, the better, you can't possibly overdress here. Past party themes have been angels vs. Devils, Blood massacre for Valentine's Day, Wicked Winter Wonderland, and Alice in Wonderland. A dungeon is equipped with bondage equipment, but most guests are more interested in dancing to the techno and industrial music, mingling, and showing off their looks. Entry $12 in advance, $15 at the door.

PADDLES

250 WEST 26TH
(SIDE DOOR NEXT TO PARKING LOT)
CHELSEA, 23RD OR 28TH ST. STATIONS
WWW.PADDLESNYC.COM

Naughty or nice, everyone is welcome at Manhattan's self-described "Friendly S&M Club" for a proper and thorough spanking. Come after fueling up and before heading home with your playmate, as sex and alcohol are verboten (although if you bring a bottle in a bag with your name on it you can leave it at the coat check). the retro 50s style Whips & Lips Café will do in a pinch for soft drinks and light snacks, but at Paddles the focus is really on the BDSM play. While it could use a lady's touch in the overall decoration, there is no lacking in equipment, with 30 different pieces of the latest high-quality bondage equipment where scenes involving everything from suspension and foot worship to being spanked or caged like an exotic bird. There are several rooms spread out over 5000ft^2 on two floors, some large and spacious, others dark and narrow. Paddles has been in business for 23 years, with a loyal and diverse following of friendly regulars (30 to 50 years old) who are happy to show newcomers around. The inclusive door policy means the ratio of men to women can often be seriously off-balance, so ladies are advised to come with their friends or partners for the evening rather than risk running the creepy guy factor gauntlet solo.

Entry $10 for ladies, $40 for men. Open Friday-Saturday 10pm-3am. Open early the first Saturday of the month from 7pm for the spanking–only OTK (Over the Knee) party. Ladies who dress like schoolgirls get $5 off entry fee. The dress code is quite relaxed in general, with all black outfits tolerated as long as you're not wearing jeans and sneakers. But why not vamp it up and dress to impress with the best of them in latex, leather or stiletto heels and a fitted rubber corset?

Private Dungeon Rental

Looking to play out your own BDSM fantasies with your partner in private? Behind Manhattan's closed doors are many fully-equipped dungeons and play rooms available for rental. Pandora's Box is one of the most famous, with themed rooms such as the School Room, Ming Palace, Wrestling Room, Medical Chamber, and the Sanctum, a replica of a 16th century church for your Spanish Inquisition scenes. Conveniently located next to Paddles S&M Club: Tel 212 242 4577 www.pandorasboxny.com

Naughty Resources

Clubs come and go, parties change venues, and new events are created at any given moment. To keep up with the swinger's scene, check out **Swing Lifestyle** (aka SLS by the regulars; www.swinglifestyle.com). For fetish and BDSM parties check **www.fetishpartyinfo.com**, **FIXE Magazine** (www.fixemagazine.com) or **FetLife** (www.fetlife.com), the most popular site for social networking and "play" dates in the BDSM scene. The **Eulenspiegel Society** (www.tes.org), a non-profit organization promoting sexual liberation, also holds events, mixers, and beginner's workshops. You can also find **flyers** for events at many of the shops listed in our **Naughty Shopping** chapter, including Purple Passion and The Baroness.

CONTRIBUTORS

Naughty New York was brought to you by...

Contributing Editor **Heather Stimmler-Hall** is a Paris-based travel writer, tour guide, indie publisher, and author of the award-winning "*Naughty Paris: A Lady's Guide to the Sexy City*" (2008). www.secretsofparis.com

Principal Photographer **Kirsten Loop** is an information architect, Neo-Luddite and mom. She has made a career out of figuring out what she wants to be when she grows up. www.loopphotography.ca

*the*BookDesigners, **Alan Hebel** & **Ian Shimkoviak**, have over a decade of book design experience. They are passionate about books – reading them, designing them and holding them after they're printed. www.bookdesigners.com

Our Team of Talented Writers

Beebe Bahrami is a widely-published freelance writer and cultural anthropologist specializing in travel, food and wine, adventure, spiritual, and cross-cultural writing. www.beebesfeast.com

Jessica Firger is a New York City native freelance writer and journalist, whose work has appeared in the *New York Times, Wall Street Journal, Daily News, Time Out New York,* and *BUST magazine.* jessicafirger.com

Leah Furman is an author and lifestyle writer who's been dining in New York City since 1994. Leah has written more than 20 books about everything from dating to celebrity biography, but her favorite subject remains dining in her favorite city on the planet.

Ronnie Koenig is the former editor-in-chief of *Playgirl* magazine and writes about sex and relationships for *Cosmopolitan*, *Redbook*, *Penthouse*, AOL and iVillage. www.ronniekoenig.com.

Mia Martina is a writer, smut podcaster, and reading series host who, after a decade in New York City, now lives in Austin, TX. miaontop.com.

Jeannette Park is a lifestyle, fashion and beauty journalist living in New York City. She has written for *WWD, New York Magazine,* Julib.com, and Modern Luxury.

Yolanda Shoshana is a multi-platform Manhattan media personality: courtesan coach, luscious lifestyle guru, blogger, columnist, television/radio host and speaker who swirls sexuality, sensuality, and sexuality. www.lusciouslifestylediva.com

Jean Tang is a Brooklyn-based travel and food writer with a talent for "word photography", and the founder of the copywriter's collective MarketSmiths. www.marketsmiths.com

Acknowledgments

A special thanks to our lovely models Maria de Jesus Castellon, Coralie Cervello, Guillaume Hotelin, Jessie C Nelson, Anna Spiewak and Christopher Waldmann for braving the exterior shoots during a particularly freezing cold New York City winter. Friends, family and fans also provided much-needed moral support, editorial assistance and advice during the long production process: Ethan G, Victoria K, Christian M, Wendy M, Lord Brett, Nalin P, Julie S, Leslie S, Victoria S, Rona T, Emily V, and my assistant Bryan Pirolli. Big hugs to all of you!

PHOTO CREDITS

All photography in Naughty New York is by Kirsten Loop except the following images:

Courtesy NYC Tourism Office: Clayton Cotterell (p 4, 64, 198), Julienne Schaer (p7, 135, 150-51, 163), Will Steacy (p 8), Alex Lopez (p10, 50, 63, 180, 265), Felix Candelaria (p12), Jen Davis (p16, 31, 60), Ben Dwork (p23), Jenny Rotner (p 38, 182), K Fox (p80), Daniel Krieger (p149, 194 top), Malcom Brown (p152, 183, 191, 263).

Courtesy The Bowery Hotel (p99-101)

Courtesy The Standard Hotel (p106 by Thomas Loof & Nikolas Koenig)

Courtesy Barney's Shoe Department (p167)

Courtesy The Baroness (p223)

Courtesy Critsey Rowe of Couture Boudoir (p233)

Courtesy The Bar Downstairs (p245)

Courtesy Lani Kai Bar (p246, 248)

Courtesy Freemans Bar (p272, 277, 281)

Courtesy The Standard Grill (p274-275 by Max Kim Bee)

Courtesy One Leg Up (p297-298, 300, 316, 328 by John Benthan)

Courtesy Rose Callahan of the Sugar Shack (p299)

Courtesy The Box (p303 by Dlink, 306 by Chris Griffith)

INDEX